POWER
OF THE
PURSE

POWER
OF THE
PURSE

Fear-Free Finances
for Baby Boomer Women

LYNN S. EVANS, CFP®

*Woman of Substance
Publishing, LLC*

Scranton, PA

Lynn S. Evans, CFP®
President and CEO
Northeastern Financial Consultants, Inc.
3 Abington Executive Park, Suite 1
South Abington Township, PA 18411
(570) 586-1064

Website: www.LynnSEvans.com
Email: lynn@LynnSEvans.com

Paperback ISBN: 978-0-9862071-1-2
Mobi ISBN: 978-0-9862071-2-9
EPUB ISBN: 978-0-9862071-3-6

Library of Congress Cataloging Number: 2014956529

Printed in the USA

10 9 8 7 6 5 4 3 2

To Dr. Linda Barrasse who, despite all the curve balls life has thrown her, continues to be an inspiration and a good friend.

CONTENTS

INTRODUCTION

That day started just like any other day. Ordinary. Same ol', same ol'.

But the way it ended changed my life.

On that particular day in 1967, I came home from high school, jumped off the bus, and looked across the street toward my house. There were three big, black four-door sedans parked in front on the street.

I knew these cars didn't belong to anyone in our neighborhood, and they certainly didn't belong to anyone in my family. I immediately felt a knot in my belly and was terrified by what I might find when I opened the door.

Trembling, I managed to pay attention to the usual "wait for the light to turn green, look up and down the street, cross the street" without really thinking about it. I was greeted at the front door by my mother who hurried me in and said, "Come on, come on, get in here. You have to go upstairs!"

I said, "Why?"

And in a very hushed voice, she said to me, "Because your father's in the dining room with the bankers, and they want us to go upstairs."

Again, I asked, "Why?"

"Don't worry about it. There's nothing you need to worry about. Your sister and brother are up there. We need to stay upstairs until they're finished."

"What are they talking about?" I wanted to know.

And at this point, she was done answering my questions, "Oh, Lynn. Just let the men do their talking about money."

Finally, I said, "Okay."

In that moment, unconsciously, I made up three important rules about life that I've been trying to undo ever since that fateful afternoon. You will see these themes unmasked in this book:

1. Women are not supposed to talk about or be included in any conversations about money.

2. Women don't have the mental capacity to understand anything about money.

3. Men know best how to manage money.

And that was the mindset of that day. All my mom's friends were raised to believe that and lived as wives and mothers with those truths.

And those "truths" guided my life for years until the mid-1970s when the feminist movement opened my eyes to the unlimited possibilities of women and money. I learned that "pink" and "green" can be the best of pals.

Too many times I have heard stories from women who ought to know better. Yet we are not taught what we need to know—and that's to know better. Our knowledge in the areas of business, education, medicine, law, architecture, the arts, nonprofit administration, and any other field of endeavor has dramatically increased in our lifetimes, but our knowledge of personal finance is still pathetic.

Unless life hands us a reason, we have no interest. It is too boring, too taxing, and not something we are willing to sit down and figure out. No time for that.

But you owe it to yourself to know when you are being taken advantage of, when you might be given a really sweet opportunity, and when to call in the cavalry. No one is suggesting you become the world's greatest authority on 401k plans or how to select the right long-term care policy or even what mortgage deal is the best for you.

I'm sure you have had moments when you wished you knew just a little bit more. After all, you are a bright, accomplished woman in so many areas of life: loving mother, awesome wife, dutiful daughter, revered mother-in-law, eccentric aunt, tops in everything. But money scares the heck out of you.

WHY MONEY?

Money doesn't scare me now, and I've rewritten those "truths" I surmised in high school. I am a Certified Financial Planner (CFP®). In the last five years, I have seen more women than ever seeking financial advice. And that's good news. We're starting to take responsibility for our financial security.

However, there are still millions (really) of women who are scared, frustrated, conflicted, and in denial about the state of their money. Most don't know where to start. Some entrusted their finances to a spouse only to find that wasn't in their best interest. Some have been widowed or divorced or downsized and no longer have the income or security they were counting on. Some have reached out to unscrupulous advisors and were burned.

We women are, by nature, worriers, and we worry about these money issues (among others):

- Health care costs and whether we're going to be able to afford health insurance when we retire

- An impending divorce and who's going to pay for the legal costs and the "upside down" mortgage

- Our investments and stock portfolio going belly up

- Our kids losing their jobs and coming home or asking us for money we don't have

- Whether we're going to outlive our income and face poverty in the later years of retirement

- Whether our 401k plans will be there for us when we want them

- Who's going to take care of us if we have a serious and long-lasting health problem

If any of these worries keep you up at night, you're in the right place.

Somebody has to do something about this sad state of affairs. (I elected myself, and you elected to read my book.) So together, let's do something about overcoming our ignorance and claim our rightful power of the purse.

Clearly you do not suffer from a lack of information available to educate you on the basics of personal finance. There are plenty of books on the shelf, on the Internet, and articles galore on the intricacies of personal financial planning for women.

I have discovered these are not enough.

Like most things we set out to learn about, the task can seem overwhelming and completely shuts us down. So in the end, nothing is gained. To go it alone can seem way too ambitious and intimidating. And our time is so valuable, we end up doing other things we think call us even louder.

So the books collect dust, the ebook downloads go unread, the printed articles go in the shredder, the bookmarked websites get deleted, and we call it quits. Our intentions were laudable but our results less so.

And now we are no better off than when we started the quest. Our ignorance is intact and the cycle continues.

WHY THIS BOOK IS DIFFERENT

I wrote this book with short chapters, packed with insights and information so you can dip in and derive value in even fifteen minutes a day. So we can fit in small chunks of information in the course of our busy days or weekends.

Plus I sprinkle in real-life examples of women just like you, so you can relate to the stories and see what I'm saying. In every chapter, mothers, wives, widows, and working women tell stories of the challenges in their financial lives and how they worked to overcome them. All of them succeeded; all of them never thought they could.

More important, I offer questions and actions for you at the end of every chapter. You can join with other women in a facilitated circle in your living room or you can read independently nestled in a comfy chair with a cup of coffee.

You may be in your fifties or sixties. You may be married, partnered, single, divorced, or widowed. You may be an engineer, entrepreneur, or an executive.

You may also be tired—putting in sixty-plus-hour workweeks, burned out, overwhelmed. You certainly don't need one more thing on your plate. You feel as if another task added to your TO DO list will push you over the edge.

You're at that point. I understand. Believe me, I have sat across from or side by side with literally hundreds of women who feel like you do.

The good news is that we were able to address these issues instead of avoiding them, denying them, or procrastinating about them in a way that they finally felt empowered, felt they were taking their financial future and independence and security in their own hands. You can feel that way too.

I will be with you every step of the way. I will share the approaches and insights and examples that have inspired my clients to take action *today* on the many different financial issues they needed to deal with. They feel so much better about themselves. They feel as if a huge burden has been taken off their shoulders. They feel more confident they can weather the storms of the future. They are reveling in being able to care for themselves.

That's what I want this book to do for you.

WHAT MY MOTHER
WOULD SAY

Do you ever worry about money?

Probably twenty-four hours a day. Join the club.

In over thirty years as a Certified Financial Planner (CFP®) who has had the privilege of working with hundreds of clients, I've observed that we all, at one time or another, feel those worries about money.

Maura called me in a panic. She was a fifty-three-year-old woman who found herself facing an imminent retirement when the company she had worked for since high school was bought out by a *Fortune* 500 company. This was good news all the way around, but the new owners thought it would be a good idea to offer some unbelievable packages to the top brass to get them out of the way for the new blood they wanted to bring in.

Maura had never had this kind of offer in her life; it would make her an instant millionaire if she took it, but she wasn't sure why she wasn't so happy about the prospect.

"It just doesn't feel right," she said. I asked her if it might be about the fact that she was uncomfortable with that much money.

"Yeah, I guess," she replied. "I feel like I won't fit in anymore with my friends and family once they find out."

"And how would they find out?" I asked.

"What am I supposed to tell them when they ask me why I'm not working anymore? And what will I do with my life if I can't work?"

This work ethic is so deeply entrenched in our lives that we rarely see the opportunity sudden wealth affords us (pun intended). What stops us from making the kind of decision Maura had to make is the lack of awareness of what money can do to enrich our lives, rather than keep us slaves to the paycheck.

Ignorance of what money can do, how it works, and how to make it—other than with a paycheck—is what holds us captive and perpetuates an ethical conundrum: what is my worth if I cannot measure it with a paycheck?

Our parents showed us by example that hard work and a steady paycheck is what creates success. For most of us, what we know of money (or don't) is what we learned from our parents. Remember the "truths" I learned about money when the bankers were meeting with my father in the dining room, causing my mother, my siblings and me to hide upstairs?

Our parents came from a different time with an entirely different set of expectations and a different interpretation of what money meant. To them, savings and investments were the backbone of success. No reason to buy new when the old thing that had worked for years could be repaired for less than the cost of a new one. Their conversations centered on whether to buy a new sofa or to re-cover the one they had. There were no big box furniture stores flooding the airways to encourage you to buy new.

Vacations were more for spending time with extended families rather than an opportunity to take a fabulous trip to the islands.

And probably the most significant change between the two generations is the increasing frequency with which we dine out at fast-food restaurants. For them, eating out was a rare treat usually reserved for special events such as birthdays that ended in a zero or "big" anniversaries.

So our parents' money stayed in the bank. And we are becoming the beneficiaries of that incredible savings discipline. Over $4 trillion of wealth will be transferred to the Baby Boomer generation before all our parents are gone. That is a huge amount of money. Sadly, that is far less than we will transfer to our progeny.

I know that my parents put all my birthday, graduation, and confirmation gift money in a savings account in the bank. As a child, I learned there were only two things worthy of that investment of my gift money: some silver dollar coins and some Series E Savings Bonds.

Now lest you think I reached majority age with a pile of money, the total was around $50. Not a windfall to get me too far, but enough to let me know that putting money away has some unexpected but pleasant surprises down the road.

And you can bet that the "money truths" you and I made from the lessons we learned as children were deeply cemented in our brains. Mostly unconsciously. I found those rules being filters for all the decisions I made as a young adult.

When I was offered a job in a city away from my hometown, I wondered if I should take the job if I had no money in my pocket. How would I pay for my rent, food, car payment, and school loans? So, without that sense of financial security, I passed on the job.

I had no experience in managing money because it was never discussed. Parents just didn't tell children about their money. But a lot was inferred. Maybe the following "truths" will sound familiar to you.

MOTHER'S TRUTH #1

→What my mother would say: Women took what was left and never complained.

Mom was always the last one on the list. The kids came first, then her husband, then her, if there was any money left. She married and had children. That was the job she was genetically engineered for. No questions asked.

So she took what fate gave her.

But somewhere in her young, married life my mom recognized the inequity of the predetermined role. And that's why she demanded that her daughters get an education—something that would prevent them from being left to whatever life gave them. She wanted them to have a choice, a say in what kind of life they lived.

She had no say in the financial decisions my father made. She detested the end of every three-year period because she knew it meant yet another new three-year car payment. Just when they finished the payments for the last car, my father decided it was time for a new one. There was never any relief.

If there was money left over—even if there wasn't—my father's required toys for his sports activities always took precedence over what she might have wanted: a new refrigerator, a new appliance, a modern couch, whatever. She always wanted practical things and mostly things for the house.

But a new baseball mitt or new golf shoes were more important. No one expected it to be any different. All her friends and their husbands lived by the same rules. It's just how it was. In a subtle way, that expectation was passed on to me and to my siblings.

→We say: Women must have a say in financial decisions.

MOTHER'S TRUTH #2

→What my mother would say: Personal finances are exclusively the domain of men.

Women have many fears about money and most of them are based on a perceived belief, or rule, that personal finances are exclusively the domain of men.

We are raised to believe that the male figures in our lives will handle all things financial so why bother to learn. If it's not my father, my husband(s), or my son(s), then some other male person will take care of it.

That's how my mother was raised and so were many of you reading this book. Yes, they might have managed the paycheck when it was given to them: they paid the bills and the rest was theirs to keep for upcoming events for the children, and if they were lucky, maybe some piece of new clothing for themselves. But the big decisions: buying a house, finding a mortgage, investing money, and getting a better job were all linked to testosterone. Having very little of it relieved us of this burden. Or so it would seem.

Despite our progress in the workplace, we still don't feel confident about what to do with money: how to invest it, how to conserve it, and most importantly, how to use it to provide financial security.

So let's begin to unravel the years and years of suppression of that part of our brain that shies away from any talk about money. Take off the blinders and the misplaced assumptions that "I just can't understand it" and replace that with some basics.

We women are not born with a gene for shopping and spending money; it is learned behavior. Let's dispense with the cliché of husbands or fathers breaking out in a sweat when their wives or daughters decide to go "shopping" and replace that notion of frivolity. Women can shop with discipline, coupons, a list, and bargain hunt. You can have your cake (on sale) and eat it too!

When you decided to ride a bike, or learn how to drive a car, or put makeup on your face, you started from a place of no knowledge. Because you committed to the result, you sucked it up and let yourself admit to ignorance as the only place to start. You made some mistakes along the way, but it did not stop you from going forward. Eventually, you did learn to ride a bike, to drive a car, and to apply makeup so you didn't look like a Halloween mask.

Learning about money is equally simple: once you get the basics down, the training wheels will just come off.

So sit back, take a few deep breaths, and let's get going. This book is designed for those who just got their permit and need to learn how to drive, so they can get behind the wheel of a car and go.

→We say: Women are capable of learning about money.

MOTHER'S TRUTH #3

→What my mother would say: Don't buy anything unless you have the money first.

First, we need to unravel the assumptions you made about money as a child. If you can remember the first time someone put a dollar bill or some coins in your hand, think about what that meant to you. If you wanted something that you really, really, really had to have, what did your parents or caregivers say you had to do to get it?

As a small child, maybe the answer was that you needed to save your birthday gifts, your holiday gifts, your "rites of passage" gifts (Bat Mitzvah or First Holy Communion, for example). And then, when you had enough, you could buy whatever it was you wanted.

You learned the value of saving for something you wanted. But you also learned it required that you had to have the money first, in order to buy things. Maybe your parents gave you an allowance, which you learned to parse out for the things you wanted and needed: money for after-school trips to a candy store or, as you got older, money to have a Coke and fries at the local restaurant with your pals, or some was put away for a sweater you really wanted. Too young for layaways, but the idea was the same.

You needed to put some of your money away for holiday gifts once you were old enough to choose them yourself for your siblings or parents or caregivers. But the bottom line for all this was that you did not buy something if you didn't have the money to pay for it, unless you had a wealthier sister or brother from whom you could borrow the money and pay him or her back at some time in the future. Or maybe not. But credit was the last resort.

If you were really pressed for something that might have had a deadline to it, and you didn't have the time to save for it, your parents might let you have it, but you were told you had to pay it back from your future allowances until your borrowings were totally repaid.

→We say: Learning about the proper use of credit can allow us to buy things without having the money in the bank first.

MOTHER'S TRUTH #4

→What my mother would say: If you need money for something, go ask your father.

The denial of allowances was often used as severe punishment for violations too horrid to be put into words: bad mouthing a teacher, failure to be home at a predetermined time, forgetting to do your Saturday chores, for example. There was a cause and effect for many actions that resulted in the deprivation of money. And that's where we learned that money could be used to control or manage behavior.

If you had parents who denied you nothing, then money took on a totally different meaning: it was simply a means to an end and there was plenty of it. Need a car? Mom and Dad bought it for you. Need a new dress for a social engagement? Mom and Dad bought it for you. Whatever you wanted, you got it. And in many cases, the money never crossed your palms.

You learned that the supply of money was endless, and you could spend it on whatever you wanted. There was no relationship between earning money or saving it and the immediate availability of what you wanted. You learned that asking for something material and getting it was a way your parents showed how much they loved you.

Both of these are extremes, but they provide us with a significant basis for what "stories" we make up about money. Those who learned about money in the "save for what you want" category versus those who learned about "money as a never-ending means to whatever you wanted" came into adulthood with quite different attitudes toward the meaning of money.

If you were of the former camp, the first job out of college was a great learning experience in many ways. You had to learn to figure out how much rent you could afford, the car payment that would fit in the budget, and how much food really cost. These survival skills and how you dealt with them form the basis of how you now spend money as an adult.

→We say: Earning your own money and saving or investing some of it can give you freedom and choice.

MOTHER'S TRUTH #5

→What my mother would say: Learn to live within your means.

If you are married, you carry the rules you learned about money with you into the relationship. If you were successful in creating a lifestyle that fit with your income, then you learned to live within your means. And you probably learned that increasing your spendable income beyond your paycheck was a matter of getting a second or part-time job or having a hobby that allowed you to sell what you loved to create.

And many of us were too early for the Internet-based businesses, but I am sure there are those of you right now who are reaping the rewards for being a top seller on Amazon, Etsy, or eBay.

The idea of increasing your income by getting promotions at work simply wasn't an option for many of us. It carried too high a price.

You would be expected to honor the same unwritten code of behavior as your male counterparts—staying late to finish a time-sensitive project or coming in early or on the weekends to get caught up. This could cause a potential wedge in your role as mother and wife. If we did stay single and honor the code, we didn't get the commensurate pay increase as our male coworkers did.

If you are someone who lives on a budget and, for the most part, adheres to it, the idea of living within your means can become a source of great value and comfort. Being in a situation where you don't know what your expenses and income will be can be disturbing.

→We say: Don't accept the limits of your salary. Get creative and find ways to make more money.

MOTHER'S TRUTH #6

→What my mother would say: Make sure you can afford to take the risk.

Implicit in both of the scenarios of disciplined budgeting or over-spending is the underlying belief that money determines your sense of happiness and contentment and the undeniable belief that your way of managing, spending, saving, and investing money is the right way.

There is no right or wrong belief about money. Period.

There are only the subconscious beliefs that you have hidden deep in your brain—the one that keeps you up at night worrying about [fill in your own blank here]:

- What will happen to me if my husband is having an affair (will I become poor if I divorce him)?

- Are the investment accounts I picked for my 401k the right ones (will I ever be able to retire)?

- What will I do if Mom needs to come and live with me (I'll never be able to take a year off without income)?

- How can we afford that new house I love (I will have to get a higher-paying job to make enough money to pay for it)?

Almost every issue, including health issues, which causes you to worry, is fundamentally based on money—and usually on not having enough of it.

Our fears are based on limitations and restrictions we put on ourselves. Several studies have confirmed what we already know about ourselves as humans. We have a greater fear of loss than a hunger for gain. Given the two scenarios, most of us will opt to resolve the former and consider the latter as a gift.

Yet, there are those who are so committed to the promise of success that the fear of losing anything just doesn't worry them. They know they will be successful.

So why doesn't the hunger for gain motivate us as much as the fear of loss? For the answer to that, we have to look at our hard wiring again. When early humans were out on the plains where survival was our most important objective, we were primarily motivated by a strong fear of death and destruction. Most of us are still functioning in a survival mode.

Here's the funny part: if you have a roof over your head, food on your table, air to breathe, water to quench your thirst, you are well past the survival mode.

A noted psychologist, Abraham Maslow, called this The Hierarchy of Needs. He discovered that as we meet our basic needs, we develop higher goals and still higher ones, again, until we reach a point of self-actualization—a state of pure bliss, a state where we want for nothing. Everything in between is the quest for this highest state of being.

But what gets in our way of achieving it, is the continued reversion to the primary state of survival. If we could break that cycle, we would all be at the top of our game, and life would be good.

→We say: Your limiting beliefs about money are the only things that hold you back from creating your own wealth.

MOTHER'S TRUTH #7

→What my mother would say: A woman can never have too much in a rainy day fund.

What does fear of loss have to do with our finances? Plenty.

In many ways, we sabotage our higher desires to save and invest by buying the next thing we thought we really, really needed, only to find that having it didn't make us that much happier.

In fact, buying that thing may lead to regret to know that we are now further away from achieving that goal of financial independence. Yours truly is no exception. We are continually fighting the urge to spend rather than save. That, too, is a throwback to our primal times when we did not know if we would be alive tomorrow so we lived for the day.

But pressure from society has taught us this old money truth.

Any way you look at it, it's a constant struggle to stay on track, to satisfy the here and now and, at the same time, to satisfy the need for future financial independence.

So rather than give you the practical solutions to this dilemma, we need to delve into the "whys" of the disconnect between wanting financial independence and sabotaging the actions designed to achieve that goal.

Ask yourself these questions:

- Why is it that you continue to spend money you know you don't have and figure that you will pay it off sometime in the future, in essence, mortgaging your future for the demands of today?

- Why do we justify the need for new "anythings" when we know we can find a newer, yet used, anything that would serve the purpose just as well?

- Why do we think we need to buy the newest trendy clothing when buying the more classic designs and adding today's newest accessory would work equally as well?

- We often don't trust each other or know our neighbors enough to even ask to borrow a cup of sugar. But think about it. If we all need to mow our lawns, why does each home on the block need to have a mower?

Part of this struggle is the belief that having stuff gives others the sense that we are doing very well financially. In other words, the more stuff you have to show, the better you must be doing. We have an aversion to borrowing or upgrading versus buying new. The latter says we can easily afford it; the former says we are either too poor or too cheap. The subtle clues we give others is what enslaves us to keep up the façade. In effect, we are reminded that our parents borrowed, upgraded, and combed the thrift shops before they would buy new. We are too proud to accept that standard, since our current cultural norms tell us that you will not be asked to join the country club or be on the "A" list of partygoers if you show any reluctance to play that game.

And as Maslow said, after satisfying our basic needs, the next level of need is to be accepted by our peers. Embracing the old values of our parents would certainly not put us in contention for country club membership! So we struggle to "keep up with the Joneses," as we like to say.

We do try to do that. What parent hasn't felt pressure to have the ultimate birthday party for their child, to outdo the last one their child attended, to have the honor of the most fun birthday party in the class? Who hasn't wanted to find the money to send their daughter to Europe for the January session so that she could travel with her friends? Or tutor your son with golf lessons so he can be the top golfer on his high school team?

You think it's just about your need to look good? Consider the message we are giving our children. Who hasn't considered tapping the 401k or the IRA to find the money to send your kids to the college they wanted to go to, rather than the college you can afford? (Here's the bad news on that one: the kids can borrow the money but you can't finance your retirement.)

There must be a way to have it all. And there is, but most of us can't consider the obvious.

We need to start thinking outside the box. Way outside the box.

Your fears are what keep you small. Your fears are limiting your ideas as to how to solve the dilemma. Einstein said he is not smarter than anyone else; he just stays with the problem longer until he figures out a solution. Start with considering that you can solve the dilemma. You are not limited to the paycheck you bring home—or the lack of one.

→We say: With the help of the Internet, look beyond the constraints of a paycheck for additional sources of income.

NEW MONEY RULES

Mother's Truth #1: What my mother would say: Women took what was left and never complained. But we say: Women must have a say in financial decisions.

Mother's Truth #2: What my mother would say: Personal finances are exclusively the domain of men. But we say: Women are capable of learning about money.

Mother's Truth #3: What my mother would say: Don't buy anything unless you have the money first. But we say: Learning about the proper use of credit can allow us to buy things without having the money in the bank first.

Mother's Truth #4: What my mother would say: If you need money for something, go ask your father. But we say: Earning your own money and saving or investing some of it can give you freedom and choice.

Mother's Truth #5: What my mother would say: Learn to live within your means. But we say: Don't accept the limits of your salary. Get creative and find ways to make more money.

Mother's Truth #6: What my mother would say: Make sure you can afford to take the risk. But we say: Your limiting beliefs about money are the only things that hold you back from creating your own wealth.

Mother's Truth #7: What my mother would say: A woman can never have too much in a rainy day fund. But we say: With the help of the Internet, look beyond the constraints of a paycheck for additional sources of income.

EXERCISE

Making money is always a tradeoff. Is it that you fear the lack of income or do you fear the responsibilities of wealth? How do you define wealth? Most people would say that it is the ability to buy what you want when you want it without consideration of what it costs. And, of course, the philosophical among us would argue that true wealth is a loving family, good health, close friends, and the freedom to move about at will.

So let's start first with your definition of wealth. Take out a piece of paper and write down all the big picture and smallest details of what your world would look like if you were wealthy, as you define it. Give yourself permission to be way out there.

Okay, the Type A personalities out there: Do the exercise now. It will help you appreciate the rest of this chapter.

If you've exhausted all the thoughts you have on the subject, some wild and crazy, some traditional, and some in between, then let's take a look at what you need to do to have all or some of that.

Did you notice that it was quite freeing to do that exercise? What was missing were the limitations you arbitrarily assign to creating wealth. No one asked you to judge whether your thoughts would work in the world you now live in or whether you were so far out there that a trip to the shrink's office might be in order. No one asked you if you could afford it, or if your significant other would approve it.

There are things on that list that you could have today. Right now. They don't need lots of spare cash, just a willingness to experiment and have fun.

Maybe you hate having to cook. Personal chefs in your town can help with that. Many franchises will allow you to select the food you want for a week. They prepare it and you take it home needing only to pop your dinners in the microwave to have the perfect, well-balanced nutritional meal. Colleges that offer hospitality and culinary arts degrees could have students who would love to prepare meals for home delivery much less expensively than an entrepreneur in that same business.

How about a desire to travel? If you worked with a local travel agency and developed an area of expertise about a part of this great world, you could arrange trips and find groups to support you in paying for your tour guide experience. You don't have to stay in five-star hotels to enjoy the areas you love to visit.

Go back to your list and find the top five activities you would do if you were wealthy and figure out how, without tons of money, you could achieve the same result.

The point is there are many ways to achieve the same result that do not require great financial resources.

Leaving our rules about money unexamined, we can end up being a victim of the thinking we learned from our parents about money. In honoring the best of their teachings, we often view our current approach to money as one of deprivation and sacrifice in favor of saving for some arbitrary point in the future called retirement. I know you know many people who denied themselves many wonderful life adventures for fear of not having enough money to retire (or for a rainy day). And then when retired, he or she died shortly after.

In order to be truly open to the wonderful possibilities of living a life we love right now, we must be willing to examine all our values and thoughts about money—those that are buried deep within us and those we can see right in front of our noses.

If you were unsuccessful in really delving into this exercise in defining wealth, then let's make that a richer and more meaningful vision by asking some specific questions to help you dig deeper. Consider the following:

- What was your first memory around money? What did it teach you?

- Who is one of your role models in life, famous or not? What do you admire about him or her?

- If you had $1,000,000, what would you do with it?

- What was your first job? What did you do with the money you made?

- Who bought you your first car? How did you feel about that car?

- What was the most defining moment in your life? What did you decide about life from that experience?

- If you were told you had only one month to live, free of pain or discomfort, and money was no object, what would you do with those thirty days?

- What resources or support systems would you need to find financial "peace of mind"?

Your answers to these questions will form the basis of your freedom from fear about money. They tell a huge story excavated from your memory and will give you some opportunities to examine all those preconceived ideas you have carried around with you for many decades. Once revealed, you can pick and choose which ones you feel are inviolate and those that you need to banish from your mind.

As a child you learned "the truth" as your parents and society taught you. Now is your chance to examine all those truths related to money and your self-worth as you live out the rest of your life. It's time to reclaim your life based on new premises and new "truths" as you define them.

No wonder we are having so much trouble figuring out who we are. There is much work to be done and much introspection to delve into. And we are figuring it out as we go along. Once again, the Baby Boomers are redefining life as we know it. The outcome will no doubt be exciting.

In future chapters we will look at how your answers to the questions in this exercise will impact the way you spend, save, and invest the money you have, all with the conscious intent of creating a life you will love and one that inspires you to get out of bed every day.

CONSIDER THIS

Our friend Maura who was embarrassed to retire early for fear of losing her friends and estranging her family did take her buyout package. Together, we worked out a plan for her life, which included significant time volunteering with the local animal shelter and setting up an anonymous matching program for donations to the shelter. She had agreed to take some dream vacations and pay for a few family members to accompany her. And she knows she will be fine financially throughout her retirement. She says she wishes she had done this sooner.

And then I met Estelle, a single woman in her late fifties. She never married, had no children, and her mother recently passed away, her father ten years ago.

She did her research and found my company online. She called and left a message that she was looking for a female financial advisor because she felt embarrassed to have this conversation with a man.

It seems her mother left her a significant inheritance she didn't really need. All her life, she had saved diligently as did her mother for "a rainy day." Despite paying the costs of caring for her mother, whom she assumed was destitute, Estelle managed to save half a million dollars in the bank and put nothing in the stock market.

"When I went to the lawyer's office to settle Mom's estate, I discovered she had an investment portfolio of close to a million dollars that Dad had created for her," Estelle told me. "She never talked about it. I don't know that she even knew what was in it, but the lawyer said the dividends and income were always plowed back into the portfolio. Why didn't she or Dad ever tell me about it? I might have taken more risk with my own money or spent it on other things during my life. I'm all set with what I need, but, boy, do I wish Mom had enjoyed some of it during her ten years after Dad died. I can't believe they never talked to me about money in my entire life!"

ACTION STEPS

- Select three things from your "definition of wealth" exercise that you would love to enjoy and create a plan to get them in the next twelve months. (Remember to think outside the box!)

- If any of your siblings are alive, ask them to recall some money "rules" your parents handed down to you verbally or by example. Did you get an allowance?

- Make a list of those rules you will definitely jettison from your life and what among the new, empowering rules presented here will replace them.

GUILT-FREE FINANCIAL PLANNING

I'll always remember the lunch conversation I had with a woman who had been let go by her company six months before.

Gerry had been unexpectedly downsized by her billion-dollar pharma employer. She hadn't even seen it coming. Even though she'd worked for them for years, she found herself without income, an aging father to support, and a new mortgage on a home she'd purchased just six months before.

She told me, "I feel so stupid. I can't believe I have so much knowledge about marketing, and I know so little about money!"

Then she went on, "I got a really cool job right out of college in entertainment marketing, had a great salary since I was in my twenties, and never thought much about it. At first, when I got let go, I decided I was going to use this time to start taking better care of myself. I joined a gym, I started eating better, and I've lost eighteen pounds. Then a friend suggested I hire a financial planner to help me get my money house in order. I never realized until I lost this job how stupid I am about money. I need help!"

Despite her fears, the Taking Care of Gerry Project (as she called it) was inclusive of this need to find a smart financial advisor to help her plan the financial aspect of her life. She promised her friend who was guiding her that she would have a financial advisor by the end of the summer. And that's where I came into her life.

I was fascinated to hear her say she was interested in finding a woman to work with because she felt she had been "talked down to" by the men who had interacted with her during her adult life: the bankers, the mortgage people, the 401k counselors, the car dealers. So she really was intent on finding a woman who could not only relate to the issues she was experiencing but also understand the emotional implications of what she feared.

Her "money truths" thus far had taught her that it was not important to her advisors to know about her fears and concerns, only to know what she wanted her money to do and by when. She felt she was being told what to do with the money, not invited to be a partner in the process.

I had always hoped this was the reason most women came to see me, but it was enlightening to hear it from another woman.

As women, we may have had little interaction with money. It wasn't until the nineteenth century that women were no longer considered property, which their fathers, and, by default, their husbands, exchanged for other assets and for elevated positions in society. The dowry was a major part of the decision about whom to wed. Families carefully weighed the advantages or disadvantages of marrying their daughters to equally but hopefully better situated men. Hence the term *marrying well*.

But along with that came the tacit assumption that all financial matters were exclusively the domain of the men in the family, and the women were not privy to that information. In addition, it was considered presumptuous and rude for a woman to ask her husband about their finances. He took a query like that as an insult that she did not trust him to manage their affairs properly.

Not only was it rude to question your husband, but it was equally forbidden for children of both sexes to ask about their financial situation unless their father willingly shared it with them. But at a certain age, the sons were taught by their fathers more by observation and interaction than by formal training about the family's finances, in the expectation that they would carry on the family businesses. And, of course, the daughters were taught the social graces so they might attract a young man of wealth, but never the skills to understand money. So the woman's ignorance of all things financial was perpetuated.

Unfortunately, we haven't come too far away from that standard in the twenty-first century. Within my generation, it was the assumption that the young men in the family were to be given whatever money there was for a college education because, after all, "the girls will get married and have children, so why spend the money?" Thankfully, there were those mothers (like mine) who thought differently.

Yet, in no class in college did I ever have a course in basic personal finance. What I learned, I learned the hard way. Still, my parents did not discuss money with me. I had my own college loans; I paid them off over ten years. I bought my own cars; I financed them. I started my own business; I borrowed what I needed from cash advances on credit cards. I found the money to do what I needed to do, but I never had anyone tell me how.

As I read and learned in the classes I took to become a financial planner, I learned how to do money management right. And I taught that to other women once I got the Certified Financial Planner® designation. There is so much more to do.

If we women knew the difference between a home equity loan and a home equity line of credit, the difference between a lease and a purchase of a car, the difference between a stock and a bond, the difference between an adjustable rate mortgage and a fixed rate mortgage, we would be so much more powerful to interact with the world. Knowledge is power.

What will that power give you?

In the short term, it will give you the ability to do the following:

- Make the right decisions on whether or not you can spend money on things you want to buy without sacrificing something else down the road

- Bounce back from the blows of unexpected financial demands: dental work that costs more than your insurance policy covers, the loss of a job, the furnace that blew up last week, the once-in-a-lifetime chance to accompany someone to a place in this world you never thought you would get to, the chance to go back to school for a degree

- Deal with whatever unexpected event or opportunity, good or bad, that can or will come up in your life

- Fend for yourself when The Bank of Your Parents shuts down

Most of all, it gives you a guilt-free attitude to life. You can spend the money now knowing you have the future covered. That is a level of emotional freedom few people have.

Recently, I met with some friends, one who had recently successfully survived a year-long battle with breast cancer. She had transformed her attitude to life, choosing to live for the moment, doing many things *now* that were formerly in the "someday" column. She explained both she and her husband had been fortunate to have had successful careers with a solid telecommunications company that treated them both well. Her retiree insurance plan covered so many things she never expected. They still had to put out some money of their own, but nothing like some friends who literally mortgaged their homes to pay for their medical care.

Now that she was given the approval of her doctors, they were planning an Alaskan cruise with their whole family for next summer, and they were thrilled they had the ability to pay for that. She did say they worked with a financial advisor for several years who had guided them well in their investments so that they could do all this. She wished she could tell more women to do the same. She was involved in all the discussions with the advisor, unlike her mother, who never knew or cared about money. She is a perfect example of the freedom knowledge can give to a woman.

And lest you are thinking, *if paying for a cruise is that woman's idea of what financial stress is all about, do I have a story for her,* know that the ignorance of money permeates all socioeconomic levels of women; the issues are the same, the numbers are just different.

In the long run, having knowledge of money will serve you in ways you can't imagine. If you knew nothing about money, consider these questions:

- How would you know how to plan for your retirement?

- Where can you afford to live?

- When can you retire? Will you ever be able to retire?

- How long will your income last? Will you outlive your money?

- Can you afford to take some trips to places you've always wanted to see?

- Will you be able to afford a nursing home if you needed it, the county home or a place more in line with your current (higher) standard of living?

- If you have grandchildren, can you afford to help with college costs?

- How much can you give to your favorite charities without jeopardizing your retirement?

When presented with money choices, we all can benefit from some financial education. It can be as simple as how to use coupons wisely to purchase food, or as complicated as paying for a trip for your entire family.

Money is money. Its axioms are timeless. In the late eighteenth century, Ben Franklin wrote, "A penny saved is a penny earned." Tithing (giving 10 percent of your earned income to others) is found in the Bible. The advice is everywhere. Money management classes can be found at every level from grade school, high school, college, to adult education classes and online. But please make sure the teacher is teaching for nothing more than the gift of sharing knowledge.

Many salespeople out there in every community use the classroom as a way to solicit new business. And then they convince you to do what you shouldn't do with your money and you're right back where you started. Actually worse: you now distrust those who call themselves financial planners and you feel even more hopeless.

See chapter 4 to find out how to find the right financial advisor for you.

ACTION STEPS

- List three things in your personal financial world you are curious about. Do some research on the web and find out at least one thing you did not know about them (401k investments, mortgage rates, lease versus buy a car, are some examples).

- Think about what your father taught you about money. Or didn't.

- Find two or more examples of what successful women have to say about their relationship with money. See if it is similar to yours.

MONEY MAKES THE WORLD
GO ROUND

I'll always be grateful to the group, Directions for Women, for recommending the book *The Millionth Circle* by Jean Shinoda Bolen, MD.

I ordered it from Amazon.com, and it showed up two days later. I was by myself on a sacred Friday night (the one night of the week I normally reserve for "down time"). I took one look at its slim size, just eighty-seven pages, and thought, *I can knock this off in one night.*

By the time I was three pages into the book, I was hooked. I was immediately intrigued and impressed with the "bigness" of Dr. Bolen's approach.

Think about that title. *Millionth.*

Her profound premise is that when the millionth circle is formed, it reaches critical mass and positively impacts not just the participants of the circle, but the society that surrounds those circles. Let me explain.

Dr. Bolen starts with an insightful story about how monkeys living on an island off the shore of Japan learned, through trial and error, to wash their sweet potatoes. One monkey decided, *I'm tired of eating sweet potatoes with all this grit and sand. There's got to be a better way. Why not wash it in the ocean and see what happens? Hmmm … tasty. And I love that salt. Makes it even better. Hey, there's my brother … I'm going to show him how to do it too.*

Well, Big Brother showed the washing technique to his friends and, soon, the ritual became a monkey norm.

Ho hum. What was fascinating was this: scientists found that monkey colonies on other islands also started washing their sweet potatoes—even though they'd had no direct contact with each other.

This phenomenon has become known as the "100th Monkey Effect." The premise is that when a significant number of people change their attitude and behavior, their culture shifts as well. What once might have been unthinkable or impossible now becomes the status quo.

Ta-da!

That's exactly what we need to do for women and their relationship to money.

All these years I've witnessed women trying to figure this out on their own. I've seen them struggle with stereotypes and traditional roles that have disempowered them. I've seen bright, talented women executives and entrepreneurs with MBAs, MDs, and PhDs, who were absolutely brilliant at their job break down and cry when asked a few simple questions about their savings, 401ks and retirement plans.

I've had women tell me they've "put off" facing their finances for years. Many have told me, "My parents never talked about money and I just never learned."

Many are deeply embarrassed about ignoring their money situation for so long. Some have delegated this responsibility to others; some have been so busy they kept promising themselves they'd look into it someday; some have given up, under pressure, surrendering their finances to family members who promised "they'd take care of it."

A common theme was these women *felt all alone about this.* They didn't know what to do or whom to turn to. As a result, they often feel intimidated, overwhelmed, ashamed, and stuck.

- They need support.
- They need someplace they can talk honestly about the topic of money.
- They need an opportunity to delve into how they feel about money and why.
- They need a gentle yet facilitated environment where they can connect with peers who are in the same boat—a place they feel heard, seen, and encouraged.
- They need a structured opportunity to discuss these issues, get information, and make informed decisions about what to do next.
- They need something to look forward to such as a monthly meeting where they can address this dreaded topic that normally gets ignored or set aside so money talks become a healthy part of their life.
- They need a way to keep the various financial issues relevant to their life front and center so they can map out specific ways to spend, save, and invest their money so it works for them.
- They need a pro-active place where they can be held accountable for making tangible progress so they have something to show for their hard-earned money.
- They need ... a Money Circle.

We women need better ways to wash our sweet potatoes. We need opportunities to talk about this topic as freely as we talk about our kids, pets, jobs, celebrities, hobbies, husbands, meals, movies, menopause, and vacations. We'll all get better results and have more fun and get more done if we do it—together.

Even more important, based on the 100th monkey effect, not only will the participants in the Money Circles benefit it is my sincere hope that these Money Circles will raise the bar on what is a basic understanding of money and how it works. And then we'll pass that on to our daughters.

As a result of the cumulative sharing and connections, I hope that women in other counties, states, and countries will also start talking about this issue, supporting each other and improving our collective relationship and results with money.

WHAT IS A MONEY CIRCLE?

Picture a warm grouping of comfortable chairs, a place that calls you to come in and sit down, a place to relax, a place that is safe, a place you can be who you are without judgment.

It's a place you want to come to, a place that makes you feel good about yourself and sharing with your sisterhood. It's a place that welcomes you each time you visit and lets you know you can say anything you want without fear of embarrassment, incrimination, shame, or ignorance.

Sounds tempting to me.

We will sit in a true circle. No one is at the head of the table or the end of the conference table. We are all equal. We are all leaders. We will not lead by fear or intimidation or by appointment. We will lead by sharing our common concerns and hopes.

The meetings will start with the sound of a soft bell. The table in the center of the room is like an altar. On the table we will place things that are significant to us: pictures or mementos of women who are alive and in our lives or those who have gone before us. We can bring into the circle the concerns we have about them or the memories of their gifts to us.

We will have a candle (flameless or real) for guidance and light and a token of our shared wisdom, and some fresh flowers to signify our love of life.

We will begin each session by checking in with the participants: how they are feeling at the moment, what pressing issues they are dealing with, and any thoughts they wish to express from the last meeting (if this is the second or later circle session).

Then we will allow the facilitator to begin setting the stage for the discussion topic of that meeting.

The facilitator will begin by posing some questions for the group either for each participant to answer individually or with a partner or in a small group.

Following each time period to answer the questions, the facilitator will ask for volunteers to answer the questions for the group or not. No one is required to speak at any time. The conversation is free-flowing and not scripted. Where it goes is different with each session and with each group.

The facilitator will close the meeting by asking each participant to offer some information on what she got out of the session that evening, be it an observation or an epiphany or something incomplete that needs to be addressed.

The facilitator will close the meeting with a verse or poem or other inspiring statement and assign homework to the participants for the next session.

The soft bell will be rung, the candle extinguished, and the session formally ended.

It is expected that all participants honor the code of confidentiality so that the space is safe. Violations of this will require a participant to be excluded from the group.

WHAT ARE THE EMOTIONAL BENEFITS OF A MONEY CIRCLE?

- Mirroring: In the exercises we do, one of the most common feedback tools is to repeat without judgment to the participant what the listener heard.

- Role-modeling: The circle members find the examples offered by the participants are useful in helping others gain confidence that they, too, can conquer the issues they face.

- Feeling heard: By virtue of the mirroring exercises, we confirm that every woman in the circle is being heard, and only one person is allowed to speak at any time.

- Witnessing: We are seeing the results of our boldness and our willingness to take risks in an area of life we don't commonly find that behavior by listening to the stories of each other especially in checking in each week with the results of our homework.

- Reacting and responding: Subconsciously, we are examining our values and their continued relevance to our lives by listening to the dialogue with others.

- Deepening: The process of discussing our strengths and weaknesses relative to money allows us to confirm and validate our own values around money.

- Laughing: Most of our fears are based on ignorance and opening up to those fears often leaves us in laughter.

- Crying: A natural female reaction, and in the Money Circles, these emotions flow.

- Grieving: Sometimes the conversation touches a place in our psyche that reminds us of how much pain and loss some financial decisions have left.

- Drawing upon experience: The women in the circle can help each other just by sharing their experiences and by example, showing others that it is not as bad as it seems.

- Sharing the wisdom of experience: We find the collective wisdom of the women in the group—the women who molded and inspired them and the promise of the younger women whose lives they will impact by example—is bigger and stronger than all the books and media on the subject.

Women approach money differently than men. That's just a fact. We collaborate and seek consensus; men compete. So if we approach money differently, then we need to communicate it differently too.

Recently, I was fortunate to participate in a Money Circle with twelve women and two men. We were all financial planners, so the commonality was both intimidating and exciting. Because we all had more than a passing knowledge of how money works, the only real issues we needed to discuss were the values we all had around money.

I remember being asked some questions that really caused me to search my soul. And these questions were designed to pull up some interesting observations of my life and my money thus far. As a sixty-year-old woman, I began to see where my own fears and failed attempts at success left some emotional scars that stopped me in my own life. Unearthing those fears left me feeling much lighter and more satisfied with what I had accomplished. I realized how others saw so much more in me than I saw in myself.

One example of my own accomplishments was how I focused on what I had left undone: the six-month gig I wanted to sign up for in the south of France to live among the locals and teach English as a second language. They saw a woman who was thinking BIG. They saw my goals as doable once other things were put in place. They gave me permission to believe in myself and admired my resilience to overcome obstacles and succeed in spite of them. What a kick!

I looked with new awareness at how my conversations about money always seemed to come from a world of scarcity and not one of abundance. How my early adulthood experiences were still in play. Probably not a good thing for a financial planner to have that mindset.

I am convinced the Money Circles can be the millionth circle that alters forever the way women relate to money, use money, and control money. What an exhilarating concept.

ACTION STEPS

1. If you could be in a Money Circle, what questions about your relationship to money would inspire you to want to join in and share your answers? Which questions would you not want to answer?
2. If you are interested in creating your own Money Circle, read the book by Dr. Jean Shinoda Bolen, *The Millionth Circle*. Remember it's only eighty-seven pages.
3. Find five or six other women, all of whom have at least one thing in common with you, and contact me at lynn@LynnSEvans.com to start a Money Circle.

HOW DO I FIND THE "RIGHT" FINANCIAL ADVISOR?

A woman sales exec called me to set up an appointment because she was concerned about her husband's handling of their investments. Carol and her husband both made six-figure salaries and had seven figures to invest.

She told me, "I out-earn him but we have a somewhat traditional marriage. From the beginning, he told me he'd 'handle this,' so I just turned it over to him. I had doubts about how all our finances were going to work out. But I knew he needed that authority, and I didn't want to emasculate him, so I conceded on the money issue."

But here is her problem, in her own words: "Over the years, he's lost more than a million dollars in bad investments. I don't want to keep working this hard forever. I don't want to travel all the time just to constantly bring in new sales commissions to put toward our retirement goals to make up for his poor investment decisions. And if I do stop all this ridiculous travel, that means we'll have less income, probably have to cut our expenses and lower our expectations for our retirement. I guess I need to have an honest talk with him about how we manage our money because we can't afford to continue to lose anymore."

Carol pleaded, "I really need a financial advisor to help me with this, because I don't know how to do this without a major battle."

I knew exactly what she was seeking and why it was so important for her to have someone to work with her. As a financial advisor, I often serve as a facilitator for the sensitive conversations that need to take place to address money issues head-on.

I know that issues around money are often the number-one reason for divorce. I know that if I do my job right, I can keep the discussions around this constructive, instead of punitive. I can turn the conversation to what *can* be done about a situation instead of what *should* have been done.

Which brings us to the question: How do you find a financial advisor who will be constructive rather than punitive?

How do you find a financial advisor who can help you focus on the future rather than finding fault? Who can delve into your needs and interests so your actions reflect what you want? Whom can you trust to help you address and resolve sensitive issues rather than avoid them?

How do you find the "right" financial advisor? And, of course, the answer is, "It depends."

Someone with $10 million of net worth needs an advisor with skills and resources far different from someone who is looking to get a better return on a $10,000 maturing certificate of deposit.

And a person who is twenty years old and starting an investment program has totally different needs from a fifty-five-year-old who is looking for retirement planning.

It is clearly not a one-size-fits-all process for selecting a financial advisor who will be right for you.

The good news is that I have developed fourteen questions you can ask yourself to increase the likelihood of finding a financial advisor who is the best match for your needs, priorities, and interests.

I know it will take a few minutes for you to answer these questions. Believe me, a few minutes now can save you hours, weeks, or months down the road and can also help you find a partner you can turn to and trust for years to come.

14 QUESTIONS TO ASK YOURSELF TO FIND THE RIGHT FINANCIAL ADVISOR

1. Exactly what area or areas of personal finance do I need help with? (Likely responses might be debt consolidation, retirement planning, college funds for kids and grandkids, mortgage refinancing, and 401k selections.)

2. Do I need a comprehensive financial plan or do I need detailed advice on a specific topic such as retirement planning or investment review?

3. Will some initial research online resolve my concerns or do I want a human being to be available for questions?

4. Am I willing to pay a fee for this advice or am I comfortable with a planner who is compensated by commissions and fully discloses what the commission(s) would be for the product(s) I buy?

5. Is this someone that I can intuitively trust? Can I trust my gut feeling about him or her?

6. Do I have the documents and other paperwork I might need for my initial visit to this planner? (Important documents to bring would be 401k statements, bank statements, bills, tax returns for the last two years, pay stubs, a list of your investments, and retirement plan information.)

7. Am I willing to act upon the advice I am given?

8. Do I want merely a sounding board to validate my existing plan or someone who will hold my hand and help me to get the job done?

9. Do I need to work with someone who will explain everything to me before I make a step or am I comfortable delegating that authority and just doing what he or she says?

10. How much interaction do I want with a planner? How often do I need to hear from him or her?

11. Do I want to interview several planners before I decide or am I okay going with one recommendation from a friend?

12. Is it important to me how long he or she has been in the business? Is a newer, younger planner more knowledgeable or does an older planner with years of experience mean a lot to me?

13. Do I expect some social interaction with my planner or do I want to keep the relationship separate from my personal life? (You're not going to become best friends (or you might), but you want some sort of rapport across the desk.)

14. Am I looking for superior returns on my money or am I looking for an advisor whose services go beyond investment expertise? (You might ask for referrals to reputable real estate agents, CPAs, event planners, caregivers, and personal coaches.)

These questions make excellent discussion points for a group or for you individually. You can find the print out on my website at www.LynnSEvans.com.

HOW TO ASSESS THE CREDENTIALS AND QUALIFICATIONS OF FINANCIAL ADVISORS

Let's dig into the likely questions you have and hammer out some answers. There is no set formula for selecting the best financial advisor; however, these brief descriptions of the different types of financial advisors can help you select one who will have the needed background, education, training, approach, special focus, and certification for your needs.

One thing planners should all have in common is a commitment to do what is best for you and not what is best for them. And that can be a hard commitment to distinguish.

Sure, all planners will be gracious and solicitous when you first meet. After all, they do run a business and are interested in adding new clients. But beyond that, how do you know whose interests they serve?

There is no definitive way to determine the integrity level of a planner, no more than there is a way to determine the effectiveness of a physician. Mostly it is a trial-and-error approach.

Consider all those who loved and admired the infamous Bernie Madoff and treated him like family. The man ended up bankrupting hundreds of people who no longer can trust their "gut" feelings about anyone, and, if they have any money left, will certainly *never* trust it again to a financial advisor.

Why do I even bring him up—especially since we're talking about how to find a financial advisor you can trust? His clients *did* trust him, or at least, they didn't ask too many questions? They felt he was a "nice" guy, and, after all, he was on the board of the Securities and Exchange Commission, and he was a high-profile man about town.

The fact that he produced an unprecedented double-digit return on his clients' investments when the rest of the advisors were barely breaking even should have been a red flag. When something is consistently higher than the norm, something is often amiss. It may be nice for "bragging rights" to talk about the "19 percent return," but that type of uncommon result ought to have been reason to investigate and think twice.

It's important to understand that the financial planning arena is still maturing. In fact, it is just beginning to create itself, just like the accounting profession did half a century ago.

In the accounting profession, there are tax preparers, public accountants, Certified Public Accountants (CPAs), Enrolled Agents, Certified Management Accountants (CMAs), and others.

Some accountants work in the public sector, some in the private domain, and some prepare taxes only from January to April from their homes.

But the one thing that creates the distinction that most readily defines the true professional is the designation CPA. Their professional continuing education requirements and ethics courses create a basis for distinction from the rest of the crowd. Passing this arduous eight-hour test is no small feat.

Once licensed as a CPA, the young professional sets out to develop a reputation in a community or in a specific business market. Often, they will develop a market niche that sets them up as a specialist in certain types of accounting areas. Because of the highly personal nature of this relationship, many people look to their CPA first for information and clarity on a variety of personal and financial issues that come up in their lives.

This pattern of developing a business reputation is similar in the financial planning world.

There are some planners trained by their primary business background. In the insurance business, the new kids on the block will take industry-taught courses and will graduate after successfully completing a thirteen-week course to be Life Underwriter Training Council Fellows (LUTCF).

For more coursework over a longer period of time, usually two years, the life insurance industry offers insurance agents the opportunity to become Chartered Life Underwriters (CLUs);

then by adding additional courses, they can become Chartered Financial Consultants (ChFCs). This designation is promoted to the general public as a financial planning degree. As is true of the industry that nurtured them, most ChFCs are compensated by commissions on the insurance and investment products they sell.

The accounting profession, too, has designations for its members who are interested in adding financial planning to their practices. This designation is called Personal Financial Specialist (PFS) and is considered a financial planning credential although it is not well recognized by the general public.

Since most CPAs do charge fees for their time on an engagement, they usually do the same for the financial planning designation as well. However, I know of many CPAs who have the PFS designation, sell products to their clients, and take commissions from the vendors whose products they sell.

This wearing of two hats—selling products and taking commissions on those products—is a source of great debate within the CPA profession. If you do engage a CPA to help you in your financial planning, you need to ask that CPA which method of compensation he or she uses.

The brokerage world (Bank of America/Merrill Lynch, Morgan Stanley/Smith Barney and many others) has both industry-required exams and optional higher education courses, which can qualify their employees as financial planners.

Each registered representative (RR) must have passed the Series 7 exam, a comprehensive exam to test knowledge of all securities, and a Series 66, a test to assure compliance with all securities laws.

These tests must be passed in order to buy or sell securities in any client's account. Additional exams, with different code numbers (Series 6, 22, 65, and others), enhance the ability of the RR to buy or sell more sophisticated financial instruments (such as options or commodities) or to be a manager of other RRs.

Then there is the Certified Financial Planner (CFP)® certificant. Yours truly holds that designation and has since 1984.

The CFP has become the designation of choice for those inside and outside the profession. There are more than 60,000 CFP certificants in the world. The CFP designation is attained by an individual who has at least three years of full-time employment in the field of financial planning or in a related field (banking, investments, insurance, among others), has a college degree, and who successfully completes the ten-hour exam offered by the CFP Board of Standards.

Once the certificant receives the designation, he or she must maintain thirty hours of continuing education every two years to keep the designation. And two hours of those thirty must be in professional ethics coursework.

Unfortunately, there is no standard for how a CFP certificant is compensated, so CFP certificants can charge fees, receive commissions, receive commissions and fees, or offset initial fees with commissions received after the plan is implemented.

There is still a rift among my CFP colleagues that centers around the preferred method of compensation. Those who are compensated by commissions believe that the commissionable product allows their clients, who cannot afford to pay fees, an acceptable form of compensation for the advice given.

Others argue that this will never truly be a profession if the method of compensation is commission. They believe that fees are the only recognized way to guarantee impartiality and fairness. They state that the commission-based compensation involves an inherent conflict of interest: whose interests are paramount when making a recommendation—the product that pays the larger commission to the planner or the product that most accurately fits the needs of the client?

And that brings us to another subculture of the financial planning profession, yet another designation: Fee-Only® Financial Planner.

The National Association of Personal Financial Advisors (NAPFA) is a fast-growing organization that raises the bar on financial planning and could truly be the eventual voice for the profession.

In addition to the requirements of the CFP Board of Standards, NAPFA demands four additional commitments to be a member: fee-only compensation, sixty hours of continuing education every two years, evenly divided over seven "core" and six "elective" areas, an initial offering of a written, comprehensive sample financial plan, and the signed pledge to uphold fiduciary standards.

The latter is best expressed using the language directly from the organization's website:

> The advisor shall exercise his/her best efforts to act in good faith and in the best interests of the client. The advisor shall provide written disclosure to the client prior to the engagement of the advisor, and thereafter throughout the term of the engagement, of any conflicts of interest, which will or reasonably may compromise the impartiality or independence of the advisor.
>
> The advisor, or any part in which the advisor has a financial interest, does not receive any compensation or other remuneration that is contingent on any client's purchase or sale of a financial product. The advisor does not receive a fee or other compensation from another party based on the referral of a client or the client's business.

So if you are looking for the real thing, you might want to check out the website (www.napfa.org) and look for an advisor who meets those standards in your area.

There are those who might have earned and still use the other designations mentioned earlier (ChFC, PFS, CFP) who are members of NAPFA, but bear in mind, they cannot be members unless they meet the stringent requirements of the organization, including the denial of commission income.

If your prospective financial planner is not a member of NAPFA, that doesn't mean that he or she is not ethical or not adhering to the NAPFA standard. I know of a few colleagues who do not feel it is important to belong to the organization for many valid reasons, one of which is political. It does mean that you must ask some deeper and more intrusive questions before you commit to working with a planner.

Those who charge fees for advice come in many different packages. Some may be members of NAPFA and some may not. Going to the NAPFA website will not necessarily capture all of the Fee-Only planners in your area, but you will get a representative selection.

They can charge by the hour for their advice, scheduled initially at no charge but with an estimate of the hours it would take to prepare a plan for you. Or they can help you decide on some smaller financial issue, such as which mortgage to pick.

Others may be a part of a Fee-Only network called the Garrett Network. This is a type of national franchise marketed to middle-income people to allow them to get the financial advice they seek for an hourly fee. You can find them online at GarrettFinancialNetwork.com.

Another group of Fee-Only planners like me charge a flat fee for the initial year of planning, based on a formula derived from a percentage of income and net worth. We offer comprehensive personal planning with a written plan, recommendations, and a checklist stating who is responsible for completing each agreed upon task and a guesstimate as to when it might be completed.

We are among the financial planners listed on NAPFA.org who charge a flat fee for our work versus those who charge an hourly fee, and there are many others like us. The listing on NAPFA tells you all of the information for any planner you would be interested in knowing more about.

The site also tells you whether there is a fee for an initial interview and allows you to see the disclosure documents we are required to submit to the government authorities each year.

For those who are compensated by commissions and fees, the Financial Planning Association (FPA) website (www.fpanet.org) will tell you what you want to know about planners who are compensated like that in your area.

After you enter your ZIP code, you can see the listing of all the planners and how they are compensated. You can find us on that site as well.

You may see that some planners are affiliated with "broker dealers" as independent advisors. Others are employees of large investment firms, such as Morgan Stanley/Smith Barney, Bank of America/Merrill Lynch (broker dealers) and a few others. These planners can also be CFPs but that does not mean they charge fees for their services.

Most of these investment advisors/planners are compensated by asset management fees for the investments they manage for you, and they may or may not charge for the planning process if they do create plans.

Those who are affiliated with broker dealers may charge fees for the financial plans but will also charge a commission/asset management fee for the investments they manage.

For many people compensated in the ways mentioned here, their primary source of income is from the investments they make on your behalf and not on the planning process. In many cases, the plan is a "giveaway" to get to the assets you own. Be very careful of that arrangement!

If your need is to start an IRA or some smaller investment such as a college education (529) plan for a child or grandchild, then you would not need the services of a financial planner. A registered rep (RR) or an independent advisor would be just fine. The commissions they receive would not be out of line for the investments they make.

My fear is that those who come into wealth, through an inheritance, a natural gas bonus, a lottery winner, an early retirement package, for example, will not see what the differences are between the types of planners I mentioned. Too many have given their new-found wealth to some unscrupulous advisor who invested it in such a way that he or she did well for himself or herself and counted on the client's ignorance to blindly accept their advice.

WHAT TO ASK A FINANCIAL PLANNER

Remember, knowledge is power. So before you take your windfall or your IRA rollover to a name with lights, consider the following checklist. (No need to re-create the wheel; I've done your homework for you here.)

You can find the print out on my website at LynnSEvans.com, so you can take them with you when interviewing a potential financial planner.

14 QUESTIONS TO ASK BEFORE ENGAGING A FINANCIAL PLANNER

1. How are you compensated? Is it by a fee and commission? Do you fully disclose the fees and the commissions you earn on every investment you make or service you offer? If compensated by fees, what is the average fee your clients have paid?
2. How many years have you been in the business? How long have you been a planner?
3. Can you give me some references of people you have worked with for more than two years?
4. What is your typical client like? Income levels, issues, investment amounts?
5. What training did you have to be a planner? What were the requirements for attaining this degree or designation?

6. How many hours of continuing education must you have to keep your degree/designation?
7. What does a completed financial plan look like?
8. What is the most important difference your work made in someone's life?
9. How many clients do you have?
10. How many support staff do you have? What are their credentials?
11. Do you have a privacy statement? May I have a copy?
12. Is there a confidentiality agreement among you and your staff? Have there ever been any violations of that agreement?
13. Do you have a copy of your Form ADV (a required disclosure form from the securities authorities)? Are there any securities violations you have been responsible for?
14. Do you have a formal contract to delineate the responsibilities of the clients and those of the planners? Does it also address a protocol to settle differences and to terminate the relationship? How long does the contract last?

There are many variations on the answers you will get to these questions, and there may be some questions I left out that are important to you (perhaps if the offices are nearby, convenient, accessible by email).

Noticeably absent is a question referencing the planner's investment performance. For good reason: the planner's average return on an investment is not the key to his or her success. The ability to meet the clients' goals is what really counts.

If you are a very conservative investor, then getting a 15 percent return on your IRA would be wonderful, but the potential for loss inherent in that kind of investment strategy might not be acceptable to you.

On the other hand, if you are comfortable with severe ups and downs, you might be disappointed with a 5 percent return, even if that is all that is required to achieve your goal for retirement funding.

If a "planner" tries to impress you with the superior returns he or she has been able to get for all his or her clients, beware. This is not necessarily a planner; this is an investment advisor. Even though a planner *can be* an excellent investment advisor, his or her primary concern must be the need to achieve the goals the client sets. Anything above that is pure gravy.

I would prefer to err on the side of underachieving on the investment returns to assure a better-than-average chance of making a goal than on the side of pushing the edge of the envelope to try to get a higher return.

Taking the latter route will also increase the chances that the strategy will fail. The need to assess a client's tolerance for risk is part of the fiduciary standard, mentioned earlier. This is way too important to dismiss lightly in favor of an advisor wanting to outperform his or her peers. Please screen prospects carefully for this type of "planner" and make sure you do or do not want that type of relationship.

Yes, some planners can do an excellent job of creating a comprehensive plan but fail to help you implement it. A brilliantly developed plan sitting on the shelf collecting dust does nothing to give you peace of mind.

You must inquire as to the degree of involvement the planner promises in motivating you to get the job done. We tell people we are the highest paid "pains-in-the-butt" and if they can't bear to deal with the constant reminders, then their money will be wasted.

It takes a lot of reminding (some will say nagging) especially in the first year to be able to check off completed action steps. And be sure to ask a prospective planner what system he or she has in place to monitor the progress of the implementation of the plan. If there is none, then walk.

Being out there on your own, with no one to account to, will guarantee procrastination, frustration, and, ultimately, failure. And that lack of accountability is often what got you to the planner's office in the first place.

Then there is the contract. As fiduciaries, Fee-Only planners are obligated to present a contract that can be no more than one year in duration, renewable at the discretion of the client(s) for each successive year, which clearly spells out the terms of the engagement, to include the following:

- The parties to the agreement
- What services can be offered by this firm
- Whether the planner is affiliated with any broker dealer
- The firm's policies regarding the sale of securities
- Protocol for filing a complaint
- Options for resolving those complaints
- Service(s) you selected
- Terms of payment for that service
- Acknowledgment of receipt of the latest Form ADV
- Detail of fee schedules for investment advisory fees
- The basis of the calculation of the planning fees, if any
- Privacy statement

This formal agreement is not required by brokers because their primary responsibilities are those of a sales agent and not of a planner.

Okay, let's switch gears because I want to make a point about financial planners.

I want to share specific ways you can take more responsibility for managing your own money starting today, starting now.

One way women jumped into this in the last couple of decades was to create investment clubs. Small groups of women did a lot of reading on the subject, scoured financial reports of companies they thought they'd like to invest in, and kicked in a few bucks to invest in stocks they felt would appreciate in value.

Many of them learned about the ups and downs of amateur investing the hard way: by trial and error. It was a step in the right direction.

These investment clubs provided women with opportunities to educate themselves and take the topic of money out of the closet. Their regularly scheduled meetings gave them a much-welcomed chance to socialize while discussing finances and gave each other mutual support while tracking their investments and celebrating their successes.

If you'd like to know more about investment clubs, you might want to check out the book *Beardstown Ladies Common Sense Investment Guide*, which chronicles the adventures of one of the most successful, enduring, yet homespun clubs.

A trained, certified, experienced financial advisor is positioned to give you professional input about how best to manage your money.

Kristen played a passive role in her marital finances for more than twenty-five years. She suddenly found herself fifty years old and facing a divorce. She really resented the financial guy her ex-husband used.

She said, "He would never include me in their conversation and spoke way over my head. After a while I just quit going and now I don't know where to start to find an advisor who's right for me."

I asked her what was most important to her in a relationship with a planner. She said, "Trust, and knowing I can ask or say anything and not feel ridiculed."

It helps to know what traits and credentials are most important to you when interviewing a prospective planner. And ladies, trust your gut. It rarely steers you wrong.

ACTION STEPS

1. Take the time to answer the fourteen questions about what you're looking for in a financial planner (you can find the questions on my website at LynnSEvans.com). Take this book to lunch with you one day and take a pen and some paper so you can write down key words of your responses.

A client told me, "This is the financial equivalent of filling out the eHarmony profile. It took me a while but it paid off because I found someone who's a real match for me."

2.   If you don't have a financial planner, find three different planners in your area who are a match for your needs that you'd like to interview. Yes, I know you're busy; however, investing three hours of your time may set up a relationship that benefits you and your financial security for years to come.

Remember, you can find options in your area by entering your ZIP code at these professional sites: www.napfa.org, www.aicpa.org, and www.fpanet.org.

3.   Ask three friends about their relationship with a financial advisor. Are they happy with the guidance they're receiving and do they feel satisfied with the value they're receiving from the relationship—and are they comfortable recommending this person?

4.   Once you've identified three options, set up in-person interviews.

Take the "14 Questions to Ask before Engaging a Financial Planner" with you to the meeting. Use them to guide your discussion. These will help you determine whether this professional has the potential to be a match.

Ask for references from each advisor. Preferably, one from a client who has been working with them for fewer than three years, and one from a client who has worked with them for five years or longer.

Before making a commitment to work with this individual, find out if you will be working with the person you are interviewing with, or with someone else in the firm. If the latter, make sure that person is there at your initial interview or at least before you sign a contract. Make sure the chemistry is there since you want to engage this person as your confidante and someone with whom you will entrust your future.

NO FEAR ABOUT BUDGETING

A nineteen-year-old woman came to see me with the encouragement of her father to get some help with investments she should consider making with her "money pots."

At first, I thought this was a quirky, funny thing for a young woman to do, in light of the frivolity and fantasy of the Internet world she grew up in. In that world, the representations of humans living in a computer-generated world encouraged a kind of superficial environment where everything always turned out just fine. No one ever had to worry about running out of resources. To find a young woman who was so reality-based was refreshing, to say the least.

After I asked her to explain the purpose of these money pots, I knew she was no child. Now that she was working at a minimum wage job, she had developed checking accounts for several different contingencies in her life: car payment, investments, insurance on said car, gifts, and clothing. She said every time she got paid, she put a certain dollar figure in each of these accounts. Some of them were fixed amounts (car payment, auto insurance) and some were specific amounts she was limiting herself to spend (gifts, clothing, investments).

Now that she had acquired all of what she needed, she was looking for some guidance on what to do with the excess. She knew the car payment was depleted each month, the auto insurance premium would be paid, and the clothing allowance would be used to purchase new clothes every six months. But she was having difficulty in allocating the money to something other than a checking account for her investments and gifts. She expected the gifts to be purchased periodically (birthdays, holidays, and so on), but the bulk would be for donations and charitable contributions.

She knew the latter should be readily available but earning something better than zero interest in her checking account. The investments, though, were a complete bewilderment to her. Her parents had little experience with investing because both of them owned businesses and put most of their money back into their businesses. What they did invest was involved in retirement plans, and she wasn't interested in those investments.

After I took a deep breath and took all this in, I wasn't sure if I should give her a big hug and congratulate her or tell her she is too young to be so serious about this and to spend some more. Then I remembered what I do for a living and chose the former.

She taught me a valuable lesson that I have obviously never forgotten.

I think of the reverse of that discipline when a young woman who was making a very good income saw me because she had credit card debt in excess of $10,000 and didn't know how it happened. She told of credit card companies sending her offer after offer to get this or that card and pay only 2 percent per month on the balance.

She used the cards, paid the 2 percent, and then found the totals kept building. She was ashamed to tell her parents, too scared to admit it to herself, and found she couldn't keep up with it. The debt became a nightmare that didn't disappear when she woke up.

How can we raise two children with two totally different perceptions about money in a world that fails to teach them anything about money? Where did one get the confidence to start on a path of fiscal responsibility and another to wallow in ignorance on a path of self-destruction? Mostly, it's all in what we teach our children by inference or example or fail to teach them at all.

The nineteen-year-old in the story was an only child raised in a family of environmentally astute parents who showed her by example the value of giving back to the world. Although she was committed to doing this by her actions as a college student, her commitment expanded to financial involvement as well. It was easier for her to see that she needed to be fiscally responsible in order to teach this to others who were less fortunate. And so her values ran her money decisions.

The other young woman with the $10,000 credit card debt was always seeing her world as a reflection of what others had and she did not. She wanted "things" to make her feel equal to her peers and to be able to participate in whatever they were doing. She did not see the connection between fiscal responsibility and self-worth. So her money (or lack of it) dictated her values.

The idea of money pots may be an exaggeration. But the idea still has merit. I would not recommend that you set up separate checking accounts for each of your monthly bills, but it is valuable to set up different accounts for more general reasons. We all remember our parents setting up Christmas clubs, vacation clubs, and other types of savings accounts. But these accounts were always expected to be consumed for the purpose they were created. They never generated any long-term results. As soon as the vacation club money was spent, you opened a new one for next year. And so it went.

As we face a future with a greater emphasis on health care, in increasing premiums, in greater and extended needs, in moving to different living quarters, and other issues, there are many things in life we cannot foresee at this point. These future expenses must have a greater priority from our income, yet it is something that has no specific dollar figure attached to it. We can calculate the current Medicare premium that will be taken from each of our Social Security checks, but we have no way of knowing what that amount will be in the future.

We know that it is possible that our parents may need some financial assistance to supplement their increasing costs on a fixed income. Yet we have no vehicle to specifically address that future expense.

We know that as long as we are able to drive, we will probably need to buy a new car. I never encourage anyone to buy a car outright since it is an asset that will lose value the minute you drive it off the lot. But we need to remember that somehow we have to have the funds to afford one every so many years.

There are vacations we want to take and financial gifts to make to grandchildren, money for anniversaries and weddings of close family and friends. The more we live, the more people we know, and the more they want us to participate in the big moments of their lives. Unfortunately, they expect us to come bearing gifts.

So it makes sense to consider these "money pots." They will be like the vacation clubs and Christmas clubs of old. How do you allocate money to these pots and what type of investments should they be in? How do you reconcile these pots with your current living expenses and retirement goals? How can you afford to do all this and still have money to live?

FIXED, VARIABLE, OR DISCRETIONARY

Let's start from the big picture first. Expenses should be considered in three categories: fixed, variable, and discretionary.

Fixed expenses will occur with regularity and in the same dollar amount each year; for example, a mortgage payment, insurance premiums, and car payments. These should total no more than 35 to 40 percent of your take-home pay (or in the case of a retired person, of your net income from pensions and investments).

If these expenses constitute more than 40 percent, there may be a temporary reason for it so no reason to run screaming into the night. Perhaps there is a short-term note you took out to repair the roof or for some major repairs to your car. This note should be paid off in a short period of time, maybe one or two years. This might push the limits of the 40 percent, but you know that it will end on some definite date in the future. (If you follow the rest of my advice in this book, you will diminish the possibility of having to take out the loans in the future!)

If you look at your fixed expenses and find that they constitute over 50 percent of your net income and it does not look as if you will be able to reduce those fixed expenses, you need to do some serious review of your spending. Did you buy the house with no down payment and take a mortgage with a variable rate that is moving up every month? If so, then you need to look at either a loan modification (and risk doing some serious damage to your credit history) or a refinancing of the loan if your credit history is good to great.

Perhaps consolidate some of the loans to have one lower payment that will last longer into the future. And if you have a big number each month for credit card payments, we need to stop right there and get rid of them. That process is worth a few paragraphs in order to get spending under control.

Credit cards are a godsend and a curse. They are wonderful to have when you absolutely have to have the money to pay for something but do not have the cash on hand. One cardinal rule in using credit cards: never, never use them personally to buy things you will consume on the spot such as lunch, dinner, movie tickets, and candy. If you don't have the money to go for lunch, dinner, or a movie, then don't go. That's harsh, but it's true. If you own a business, then those are considered business expenses and are fine to put on a card, as long as you pay the card balance off each month.

On a personal level, the cards are fine to pay for those services and goods you consume if you pay them off each month. The devastation begins with the balance that keeps moving higher each month you fail to pay off the transactions you put on the card that month. And the ease with which the credit card companies allow you to pay "just the minimum" to keep your line of credit open is a further seduction to the uninformed.

At some point, the minimum is too great to pay and the ugliness of credit cards gets in your face: the calls at all times of the day and night to determine when you are going to make the payment, the threats from the collection agencies to put this on your permanent record, the continuous game of pass the ball to the next dunning agency who hopes to be the one to finally get you to part with your cash and pay at least some of the balance owed, to the hassle of trying to provide proof of your payment to the credit rating agencies and get the bad news off your credit report.

There is a whole underworld of people whose livelihood is attained by trying to collect debt. And they are ruthless.

What most people fail to realize is that all transactions on a credit card will fall into one of the three categories of expenses mentioned earlier (fixed, variable, and discretionary). So instead of seeing a credit card payment as a line item in itself, start looking at where you should place these purchases in the three categories. Then you will see how you are really spending money.

Let's look at the next two categories: variable and discretionary. Variable by definition are expenses that you will need to pay but the dollar amount will vary by your particular usage of them and the time of the year. For instance, if you have a home with gas heat, you will spend more on heating costs than someone who uses wood pellets to heat their home. So each of you will have a line item for heating, but it will vary in the extreme. It also will vary depending on the square footage of your house or apartment and whether you pay for your utilities separately.

We know we need heat and, for some, air conditioning, at different times of the year, but how much we consume will depend on where we live and our health issues. I think you get the picture. Variable expenses will usually consist of utilities, food, clothing, transportation, and gasoline, and others. As a class, they should consist of no more than 35 percent of your net income.

And discretionary is where you define your unique lifestyle. These are expenses we allocate to travel/vacations, pet care, personal care (haircuts, manicures, massages, for example), subscriptions, activities (gym fees, tennis, dance lessons, yoga classes), gifts, charitable contributions, and others. If you can live comfortably within this remaining 25 to 30 percent of your net income, then you will be fine.

Allocating some money specifically to your money pots will work. In effect, you are already doing so by allocating your expenses to one of the three categories. But we will need to up the ante if you want to add some pots as we discussed earlier.

The money to contribute to these pots will be from one or more of your discretionary line items. If you have already started to allocate an amount to travel or for vacations, then you have one of those pots. If you are making a car payment, you already know how to live with an ongoing payment for a vehicle. And your transportation pot is accounted for in the variable category when you pay for the gas each week or month.

The following chart is helpful in understanding the three types of expenses and how to allocate funds to accomplish all you want to do or have.

LIVING EXPENSES WORKSHEET

FIXED	Monthly	Quarterly	Annually
Home Mortgage / Rent			
Home Equity Loan			
Second / Vacation Home			
Auto Loan / Lease			
Other Loan(s)			
Life Insurance (Client)			
Life Insurance (Spouse)			

FIXED	Monthly	Quarterly	Annually
Disability Insurance			
Medical Insurance			
Homeowner's Insurance			
Other Insurance			
Property Taxes on Second Home			
Alimony Paid			
Child Support Paid			
Professional Dues			
Other			
Other			
Total Fixed			

DISCRETIONARY	Monthly	Quarterly	Annually
Home Maintenance / Repairs			
Yard / Pool Maintenance / Repairs			
Entertainment			
Vacation			
Club Dues			
Restaurants			
Subscriptions / Newspapers			
Animal Care			
Personal Care			
Gifts / Birthdays / Holidays			
Allowances			
Charitable Donations			
Unreimbursed Business Expenses			

DISCRETIONARY	Monthly	Quarterly	Annually
New Household Purchases / Furnishings			
Other			
Other			
Other			
Total Discretionary			

Now that you've done the hard work, it's time to see where you stand. Please convert all the expenses to annual (quarterly times four, monthly times twelve) and enter the total numbers for each category in the following three boxes.

Total Fixed		%
Total Variable		%
Total Discretionary		%
Grand Total		100%

Next step: Divide each category total by the Grand Total and you will get a percentage. Round it up to result in only two digits. Enter that number in the box next to each total.

Of course, it would be nice if all your expenses were monthly and you knew in advance what you would have to pay for the month.

But wait a minute! Some of your bills can or must be paid quarterly, semi-annually, or annually. So how do you fund for those expenses when your "budget" calls for a monthly figure?

Enter the over/under money pot. This is a separate account linked to your regular checking account. Once you complete the Living Expense Workbook, you will be able to determine an average monthly expense number. Since all of your expenses will not need to be paid every month, some months will appear to have a surplus of cash and others not enough money to pay the bills due that month.

In those months where you have an excess, you will move the extra money into the over/under account. Please resist the temptation to blow this "bonus" on something you really, really, really wanted, but no. It is merely money that is to be deferred to the over/under money pot until the bill comes due, such as an insurance premium.

If you can arrange to pay that bill once a year, by chopping it up into twelve monthly increments, in your over/under money pot, you can save yourself at least 8 percent in additional fees for paying it annually rather than monthly.

However, if you set up the payment to the bank or insurance company (or whatever vendor will allow it) to be automatically deducted monthly from a checking account, you can generally avoid this 8 percent interest charge. Manually writing a check monthly or using an online bill-pay arrangement monthly does not afford the same savings. If you have trouble with the idea of an institution dipping into your checking account once a month, then defer the money from your checking account each month to your over/under pot and then transfer it back to your checking account when the annual premium is due.

This arrangement will be fluid. In some months, there will not be enough in the checking account; in others, there will be too much. As long as you have the checking accounts linked, you can send the excess to the over/under pot and move it back in reverse when the accounts are low. (One of my clients has figured out how to do this efficiently using Quicken.)

It is more a habit than a handcuff. Like any habit, once you get into the routine, it becomes a no-brainer. You will find that you have less guilt, less apprehension about paying your bills, and more freedom to make choices than ever before within the discretionary category of spending.

It would be nice to allocate money to a great vacation and know that, when the time comes, you have the money already in the account rather than put it all on a credit card and spend twice as much paying it off just about the time you are ready to take another vacation. That is a much-repeated cycle in this country because too few people know about the money pots.

But the toughest and most elusive challenge is the health care pot. We don't know what costs we will be responsible for individually until the health care issue in this country is worked out. Yes, we can buy Medicare supplement coverage and we know what the out-of-pocket expenses cap will be, but will it remain the same in the future? Will the medication we now take be the same medication we will need in the future and will we need to add to that list of meds if an unknown health issue pops up ten years from now?

There is no way of knowing any of this, but if we deal with what we know now, we can include in the fixed category the amount we will have to pay for the deductible and for the "donut hole" in Medicare prescription coverage. It will go into the over/under pot until we need it.

On a larger scale, depending on your age, you can pay for long-term care insurance to help or to cover fully the cost of assisted living and/or nursing home care. These premiums are not cheap, and the costs keep rising. Having the coverage will help mitigate the amount you will have to pay from personal assets and leave more of your assets to your heirs.

You can be sure that the costs and the demands of Baby Boomers will increase as more and more of us need this coverage. And the insurance premium costs will go up.

There is no provision in the federal budget for that upcoming monster of long-term care, because Medicaid is managed by the state in which you live. If you are a resident of the state in which you seek care, then the rules of the state govern. And if you live in a state with a disproportionately high population of Baby Boomers, the possibility exists that the state will not have the money in its budget to pay the independent owners of the nursing homes. Guess where they will come looking to pay the costs?

If you have long-term care insurance, you can breathe a sigh of relief. And if it has a cost-of-living increase in the benefit, you can take a deeper breath. I can't write enough about the need for this coverage, and I want to make clear the fact that I am not compensated at all by any insurance company or carrier to make this statement.

If you are under the age of seventy-five, get it. And look for coverage that is tax deductible. Most of it is. Having your children buy this insurance is an even better idea. They can pay the premium, take the tax deduction, and know that their inheritance is secure.

Believe me when I write that the state governments realize the impact we will have on the state budgets when we dramatically increase the demand for the services of in-home health care, assisted living, and nursing home occupancy. They are willing to give you, or whoever pays the premium, a tax deduction to buy the insurance. The tax deduction is better than paying the cost of care for several years.

As to taking care of and funding care for your parents, you and your siblings, if you have any, should consider a conference call or a family gathering of some sort to determine how much your parent(s) need(s) to stay in their homes as long as they are capable of doing so. It may mean a shorter vacation, postponing that new couch in the living room, or foregoing the completion of that second bedroom. But you need to fit that in. If you can all agree on an amount that will work, maybe disproportionately among you, then you will at least know that you have budgeted something for that purpose.

If your family dynamic is such that you cannot have this kind of conversation, then look at covering these costs yourself. Is it unfair? Yes. But it will be easier to put the money aside now for some time in the future if you need it, rather than be forced to do so at a time when you cannot afford it.

If the need will be something like $500 per month, then start now to do without half of that per month and see how you can fit in the remaining money. For instance, if you did not eat out as much and could save $250 now, then the goal would be to fine tune the remainder of your variable expenses, such as clothing or gifts, to allow for the other $250 in a few months. Maybe the next car need not be as high on the totem pole as the one you have or a used car of the same variety might work as well.

Let's look at the down payment money pot. Most people are under the impression that renting is a waste of money. That is a money value passed down to us by our parents.

There is in fact nothing wrong with renting, as long as it carries with it an equal commitment to save/invest to substitute for the equity (equity is defined as the difference between the current sales price of the house minus the outstanding loans) most people build up in a home.

If in our current environment, your credit is not the best and you cannot afford to be in a house because the total cost of the monthly mortgage is too high, then try to defer whatever money you might be able to afford toward that goal into your down payment money pot. At some point, the funds you accumulate will be available for a minimum down payment, and you can then assess if you want to take on the additional costs of owning a home. If you decide not to take the leap into home ownership, then you can relax in the knowledge that you have the money saved and can do other things with it.

As a renter, the leaky faucet, the worn carpet, the malfunctioning furnace or loss of air conditioning is not your problem. The cost to repair those things can run into the thousands of dollars. Do you really want to forgo the vacation to the islands next year in order to pay for those costs as a homeowner? If there is a leak in the water main and the responsibility as a homeowner is yours to repair it, wouldn't you rather have the landlord assume that cost, or would your new car money pot have to pick up the tab?

On the other hand, owning a home gives you the opportunity to withdraw funds from the equity in the house, called a Home Equity Loan or a Home Equity Line of Credit. The former is a fixed loan, which you pay like a car loan over a fixed period of time with a fixed interest rate. The latter is a loan that allows you to borrow what you need up to a maximum amount with a fluctuating interest rate, and you are only obligated to pay the interest each month. The latter is more like a credit card—they set the borrowing limit and you only need to pay a minimum each month. But you will have to pay it off, usually at the end of ten years.

So if you really needed a new roof, a new sidewalk, a new furnace, or you wanted a new kitchen, a new bathroom, you could borrow the money from the equity in your home and pay it back over time. Many people have used Home Equity Lines of Credit to borrow money to pay for college tuition. While I can't recommend it, the practice is increasing in popularity since so many parents have failed to plan for college costs. But assuming you are a Baby Boomer, your college education obligations are probably in the past.

The down payment money pot should be in the vicinity of 20 percent of the value of the house you would like to buy. Then add another 3 percent for everybody's fees and expenses (collectively called "closing costs") and you are ready.

If that seems like a number so far out of the realm of possibility for you, consider investing the money so that it earns more than zero percent in a money market fund. Tell your investment advisor that you will need the money in a few years so that he or she will not invest it in anything with a great degree of risk to the principal. That way, the earnings on the investment will allow you to get there quicker.

You will need to determine with a mortgage consultant what price range you can support in a mortgage. To do this, the mortgage consultant will ask you for information on your salary, copies of your income tax returns, and a simple net worth statement (what you own minus what you owe).

Once that is reviewed, he or she can tell you how much house you can afford. Given that number (and go to the high end of the range), you can figure out how much 23 percent (down payment and closing costs) of that is and start putting it away. If you can't do that, then you will need to prioritize your spending to see where you can cut back. Then consider the possibility of owning a home as something not doable in the next few years. Who knows? Different scenarios occur in life and to write it off as unattainable forever is foolish.

Your 401k money pot is a no-brainer. Given the opportunity to have a percentage of your income deducted from your paycheck and directly invested in a well-balanced investment portfolio is an opportunity you can't pass up. First of all, you will learn to live on the net amount you receive each paycheck so the money cannot be diverted elsewhere. Second, it can reduce your tax bracket so you actually end up with more money after taxes. Third, your employer is obligated in most cases to match some part of your contribution, so you get a return on your money up front before it is actually invested in stocks or bonds. Run, don't walk, to get in on this chance to save and invest!

Even if you can move only 1 percent of your money into the 401k plan, and your employer matches 1 percent, that is an immediate return of 100 percent on your investment! That's tough to beat.

If you are already retired, then keep the same discipline and move that money into an investment account or to a Roth IRA for the future. You will not get the tax deduction a regular IRA gave you, but you will get the benefit of the tax-free accumulation of the money in the Roth IRA.

Developing a habit of investing money could be considered your rainy day money pot. It need not be invested in something that will fluctuate in value, but a simple money market fund with whatever interest rate is better than not saving at all. Most financial advisors would tell you to stop putting away money in the rainy day money pot after you have accumulated about three to six months of living expenses. Since you already did the Living Expense Worksheet (wink, wink), you already know what that number should be.

Your vacation money pot is really a way to allow you to take one or more vacations per year and not worry about the financial stress of doing so. It will allow you to set aside money in an interest-bearing account (like a money market checking or savings account), which will give you the funds you need when you want them to pay for the trip(s).

For those who are interested in getting rewards points or frequent flier miles, book the trip on the credit card to get the points and then pay it off with the funds in your vacation money pot. That method does double duty for the same money. It could help you pay for next year's trip by using the points to pay for the airfare, hotel, and car. The cost for this rewards program is usually about $75 per year, so the net effect is a real win-win for you.

The amount you will need to put in your vacation money pot is really a simple math computation. If you know that you will need about $2,000 in twelve months, then you will need to set aside about $167 per month. That assumes no interest is earned on the money. The interest, if there is any, will help you to either get a head start on next year's vacation or can be used to spend while at the destination.

But in all cases, do not assume the interest will help to pay for some of the costs. As this book is written, the interest rate is effectively zero, so learning to live with no benefit from putting money in a money market fund is quite helpful.

The new car money pot is for those who are interested in having the down payment for a new car or in having the money to spend on a used car. As explained earlier, there is no reason to pay cash for a new car because its value will diminish the moment you leave the car lot.

To lease a car, which is effectively another fixed expense payment, is not a bad idea if you are a city dweller and will use the car only on weekends or at least for fewer than 10,000 to 12,000 miles per year. Anything more than that, the bell tolls for thee at the end of the lease.

If you exceed the total mileage, the cost is steep, usually around 10 to 15 cents per mile over the limit. That can add up to a hefty bill when you least expect it.

For many, leasing a car creates a merry-go-round of leasing that never ends. It works like this: you bring the car in at the end of the lease and find that the mileage overage comes to about $600. You did not expect to pay at the end of the lease, you merely wanted to drop off the car and lease a new one. But if you don't have the extra $600, the dealers often add it to the new lease and you end up paying over $1,200 for that overage once it is added to the new normal lease payment. And so it goes. The next car has an overage, and it is again tacked onto the lease payment and you never get ahead.

So if you expect to have the car for no more than three years, and to put on only the number of miles you signed up for, then leasing may be the way to go. There are plenty of websites that will allow you to do the math. You can enter the lease payments versus the cost to buy the car outright and see what makes sense.

If you decide to buy a car because you expect to put more than 35,000 miles on it over a three-year period, then the best way to do this is to borrow the money under a home equity loan and pay your house back, instead of a bank or credit union. If you can get a home equity loan (assuming the value of your house and your credit rating allow you to do so), it is preferable to getting a loan from a banking institution.

If the loan comes from a banking institution, once you pay off the loan, you have a three-year-old car that has diminished in value from the day you bought it. If you do the home equity loan, you now have a three-year-old car and equity built up in your house. I would prefer the latter.

Regardless of how many of these money pots are relevant to your life, PLEASE REMEMBER THEY NEED TO BE FUNDED AS THOUGH THEY WERE FIXED EXPENSES. You will note

the Living Expense Worksheet has many line items called "other."
That's so you can put in the names of your money pots.

The one called over/under is not an option. This one must be
put in the fixed expense category and is to be funded every month.
The others will be determined by your lifestyle and your expected
life situations.

Carolyn was going through a divorce after twenty-five years
of marriage. She reached a point in her marriage and in her life
where the hypocrisy of the happy marriage was more than she
could bear. She was so eager to get out of the marriage and get on
with her life in a more authentic way, she was willing to give up
almost anything to buy her freedom.

It was her wish to stay in her home, a place she had built to her
expectations to include the room she loved the best, her kitchen. It
was the place she associated with great creativity and love.

Her dominant concern in the settlement was trying to keep
the house and fund her retirement so she could live the rest of
her life in peace. She expected no man to rescue her, and she was
really looking forward to a life of grandchildren and gardening
once she retired.

She asked me to help her figure out how to make it all happen,
knowing full well she might not be able to have it all.

I used the Living Expense Worksheet to create, as close as
possible, the total living expenses she would incur in the next year.
The numbers came in that she would be able to afford to stay in
the house.

But if she did, the retirement picture was grim. She would have
to work for the rest of her life unless something outside the box
allowed her to stay in the house and retire comfortably. Being the
practical person she is, she replied: "I know it will be impossible
for me to work for the rest of my life. I don't really want to. I have
given my life to the care of others for so long, I am now claiming
my own time for me. So if I have to sell my house and buy another
one for less value, I will. And I will take the money I make on the
sale of the house and invest it for my retirement."

I was so uncomfortable telling her this, because I wanted her to have it all. She could see the disappointment in my face and the frustration with which I told her the bad news.

With tears in her eyes, she said "Don't be upset! I knew this was a possible outcome, but remember what I told you: my freedom is more important to me than that house. I'll find another place to live and it will be better than this."

She was more my heroine than she would ever know in accepting the reality of her situation and not trying to do what was right for everyone else.

ACTION STEPS

1. Complete the Living Expense Worksheet. (Come on, did you think I would let you off the hook on that one?) You can find this on my website, www.LynnSEvans.com.
2. Consider which money pots are important to you and add them to the fixed expense category.
3. Set up your over/under money pot checking/money market account and link it to your checking account.
4. Use the Living Expense Worksheet to record your monthly expenses every month and see if you need to transfer money out or into the over/under account for the next three months. (Start to make it a habit.)

NO FEAR ABOUT RETIREMENT

Ted was one of my first clients over twenty-five years ago. He, his wife, and I became close friends. We talked about his retirement when we started the planning engagement. We never thought we would actually see the day it happened.

Ted and Marlene were avid savers. Despite their professions and outstanding business success, they never displayed their wealth. Always bought used cars, rarely took vacations other than to visit relatives, taught their children to save and invest early in their lives. My concern was that they would have a huge stockpile of invested assets, the ability to retire "early," and be unable to get up every day without an automatic trip to the office.

Ted was happy to begin gradually reducing his hours over five years leading up to full retirement, but Marlene just could not give up her routine. As a legitimate offer to buy the business presented itself, they could not pass up the opportunity. So they completed the sale and found themselves in retirement with so much more to do. They never imagined how they had worked so diligently for so many years.

Ted has been to classes at the local community college and has learned basic plumbing skills, which he uses to good purpose in their house. Marlene is becoming a gourmet chef, specializing in French cuisine. They travel to visit friends and relatives in all parts of the country and find their time is so filled up they said they might need to "go back to work to get some sanity."

For a growing number of middle-aged people, retirement looms as a time of extreme boredom that's about as exciting as watching paint dry. For some in the Boomer generation, this phase of life is being viewed as a curse, not a blessing.

The definition of retirement has changed so much in the last twenty years that the old clichés about retired people, as we knew it from our parents' examples, no longer fit. To sit around and vegetate for twenty-four hours or to play golf every day for 365 days, or to babysit your grandchildren five days a week gets weary. It has no passion, no fire, no incentive for getting out of bed in the morning.

What Boomers want is a next phase of life—something that moves us to want to leave behind a way of life that bores us and makes us feel trapped. It should be a time for renewal, for freedom, for doing the things that we could only dream of while working for a living. And that does not equate to a life of pure leisure.

True to the lovely pictures on advertisements for "Senior Living Communities" with shuffleboard, golf, tennis, bridge games, and oh so much more, recent retirees will often say, "I've never been busier. I don't know where the time goes!" But does "busy" mean "meaningful"? Mostly it does not.

There are those who have found something to do in retirement that is mildly amusing, maybe momentarily fun. But when there is no sense of contribution, no sense of making a difference, no sense of accomplishment, "fun" becomes your job and you look for something else. There is no satisfaction. Something is missing. Sometimes it's a nagging feeling, something we'd rather not verbalize.

It's no mystery then that those of us who are looking at retirement, as our culture now defines it, are feeling somewhat fearful. After the first six months of playing golf or tennis every day, visiting the children in all parts of the country, visiting friends who have moved to retirement communities, what's next? Clearly there is a sense of, "How long can I keep doing this before I find myself wanting to go back to work?"

Working provided you with social contacts: a never-ending list of networking contacts, sales leads, colleagues, team members, professional association members, those you reported to and those who reported to you. When you lose the social contacts you had at work (some very helpful, some very trying!), you lose a sense of belonging.

People, by nature, are social animals. From the clerk at the newspaper stand to the barista behind the counter at your favorite coffee house, you may not have known them personally (or maybe you did), but the loss of social contact even that insignificant is scary.

The promise of a routine gave your day a sense that life went on. Whether it was the train to the city, the bus ride into town, the drive along the freeway, or some other form of transportation, the same faces surrounding you, the cup of coffee at the nearby Starbucks, the deli around the corner for lunch, the four o'clock meeting every Tuesday, you had structure. It served you well by promising a sense of comfort and all was right with the world.

You perpetuated that routine each weekend with trips to the dry cleaners, car wash, and food shopping. One of those two days might have found you in a place of worship with yet another group of familiar faces. When you had moments of sickness or injury and you were homebound, and you couldn't follow your normal routine, you became anxious, a little edgy, and slightly uncomfortable. Once you could catch that train or bus, or drive the car, you felt as if you belonged again. As you near retirement, you see it as a time that takes away this routine for the rest of your life. Very unsettling ...

Of course this all presumes you loved, or at least liked, the work you did and the people you worked with. On the other hand, this flight to a life without those who made your life miserable could be a blessing. But either way, how do you now fill the time?

Can you fill that up with volunteer activities? Maybe. Once you start the contribution of time to your favorite cause(s) you will again fall into some type of routine. It helps. A lot. But is your contribution accurately matching your skill level? If you come in to help address envelopes and answer the phone and you were a former head of operations for a major company, you might soon feel empty and underutilized and you may do more harm than good for your favorite cause and for yourself. Volunteering for the sake of volunteering has its drawbacks as well.

How about that healthy paycheck or the tidy early-out package your employer offered to entice you to leave? The former is tough to give up, and the latter is tough to pass up when you consider retirement.

Most Americans do not have enough money in their 401k plans or pensions to support their current standard of living. Some thought they had what they needed until the stock market slide of 2008–2009 wiped it away.

If you did retire now, what kind of lifestyle would you have to settle for? Would you be able to do the things you had in mind, like the trip to Europe to see where your ancestors came from, or the once-in-a-lifetime cruise to somewhere exotic, or that vacation home in a place you've dreamed about for years? Maybe or maybe not.

If you postpone retirement for a few years, is that a good idea? Will your money recover in two or three years? Who knows? But even more frightening, what if you are forced out because of cutbacks and layoffs or because of the pressure from younger, new blood that wants to rise to the top?

REALIZE YOUR RETIREMENT DREAMS

So many questions and no definitive answers. I might suggest that you are looking in the wrong place. The answer to the realization of the retirement dreams you've been postponing lies in you.

We plan for the advent of college for ourselves and for our children with deliberate intent. We review curricula that might appeal to us or to our children and then we look at the tangential issues of a potential choice: the distance from home, the tenure of the professors, the probability that our child or we would have grades high enough to get in, the availability of financial aid, the dormitories, the location of the campus near inner city or in a rural setting, the tuition, the meal plans, the ratings of the college versus others of its type, the public transportation available, the internship programs, the involvement of the alumnae, and others.

When we plan for retirement, we just want to make sure we have enough money. Retirement as we knew it was always an economic event. Do you have enough money to do it or don't you? If the answer was yes, then you announced your retirement and had the congratulatory farewell dinner.

If your answer was no, then you had to fret about the conflict of staying at a job you detested but had to do until you did have enough to retire or you opted for a lesser lifestyle and pulled the plug anyway.

But answering the question of "do I have enough" never asked "for what purpose" other than maintaining your current lifestyle. What would you like to do in retirement? Most people will have a good fifteen to twenty years of retirement—some more, some less.

If we knew how long we were going to live, the numbers part of the equation would be really easy. But given the uncertainty of medical and health issues, stock market ups and downs, how will you ever know if you are going to have enough to retire or if you will outlive your money?

Let's take a new, more responsive approach to retirement planning. First, let's lose the term. Borrowing from a master on this subject, Marc Freedman who wrote the book *Encore: Finding Work That Matters in the Second Half of Life,* I prefer to consider this time in our lives as Freedman does, as the Encore years—the third age of life.

Rather than a life of complacency, resignation, seclusion, and the potential for depression, the encore stage can be the most rewarding and exciting time of your life. It's all in how you view it. Yes, there will be health challenges, boomerang kids, parents that require more of your time and care, and many other unpredictable situations that show up when we get older. But so what?

When you look back at your childhood and young adulthood, we had major problems then too. Once we were independent of our parents, we had career issues, dating problems, weddings, children, job losses, divorces, mortgages on new homes, job transfers, and fill in the blank. Somehow we survived them all. So why should this third stage of life be any different? It will be something that will not come quietly and will not go gently into the night.

Let's start with a new mindset. We are taught to think in linear terms: 1+1=2. How about ½ + 1 ½ =2? What's different, you ask? Lots. If we can learn to think outside the box and treat retirement with as much planning as we do our next summer's vacation, there is an incredible world of opportunities for Boomers if we will take the time to look.

The problem is that most of us have no idea what a successful and wonderful encore age looks like. From Mitch Anthony's book *The New Retirementality,* an ideal scenario is one that includes some participation in all of the following areas: recreation, spiritual practice, physical exercise, intellectual stimulation, emotional attachment, good health practices, friends, giving back to others, community and others. But you'll note that doing nothing is not an option!

By combining several of these areas in one or two activities, you can add to the probability of success. Anthony offers this strategy in the use of a wheel. Each spoke in the wheel creates a border for one of these major areas of life that we should include in our plans for the encore age. He asks us to consider what percentage of our time is spent on these areas now, and how that would look once we enter the encore age.

When you see graphically how you spend your time now and how those allocations of time will change, you begin to see where you want to put your efforts to increase the time you spend on certain areas and lessen the time you spend on others.

For instance, time with family might now be much lower than you want it to be when you leave your current employment and the "working" area of life will be less. You will note that working is not defined as time spent with financial compensation but it could. Since more of us are too afraid to leave the paycheck behind, working in "retirement" is not a bad thing. It could be the result of a new career or being self-employed. But if you look at which areas you want to increase your time commitment in your encore years, you will find the areas you need to focus on to create that life you will love.

On a more in-depth level, you can enroll online for a series of tests designed to focus your attention specifically on those career choices you can make for the third age. Consider a site called Revolutionize Retirement (www.revolutionizeretirement.com) by Dorian Mintzer. Then once you have the testing done, you can work with an independent coach who can personalize the process and give you a life you can't wait to get started on.

For some, the areas of intellectual stimulation, giving back to others, and community can be nicely integrated with a new career.

To design this new life successfully, you must suspend for the time the belief that you can or cannot afford it. If you take some time to consider exactly what the new life looks like, you will be surprised at what the world will deliver to your doorstep. But be careful; you get what you wish for. So make it really, really good.

The first place to look is by answering the question, "What no longer fits?" Make a list of the things you know you have outgrown. Maybe it's your current living quarters.

- Is your house too big or have too many floors?

- Have you been in the same place for over twenty years?

- Is your neighborhood filled with older people? (Statistics show that being around younger people and children helps to keep you young.)

- Would you prefer a more rural area with lots of space or do you want to live in a city with services within walking distance?

- Do you want to live closer to your children and/or grandchildren?

- Do you want to live in a warmer climate or do you love the extremes of the four seasons?

- Do you want to have two smaller places, one in the warmer climate for winter and one in the cooler climate for summer?

- If you have a pet and you intend to keep a pet, will the new residence allow for animals? How important is that to you?

- Do you prefer something new, relatively new, or are you a fixer-upper person? If you don't have the skills to fix or repair, will you learn how to do it, or would you prefer to hire someone to do that?

- Do you want to live in a townhouse development with common walls? Or do you want a single home on its own piece of land?

The more specific you make your ideal living quarters, the easier it will be to find it.

I met a woman who was terribly perplexed about giving up an apartment in New York in a rent-controlled area. She had grown up with parents who were from the Depression era and cautioned her to spend little and be happy with what you had. The apartment was old and she hated coming home to it but her parents' words kept ringing in her ears. She finally realized that she could easily afford a new condo with all the amenities in the same neighborhood she loved. She resolved to start looking for a new place and her mood immediately lifted. She realized how trapped she had been by a belief she was not even aware of.

EXAMINE WHAT YOU LOVE TO DO

How about your current job?

- Do you do it because it has familiarity or because you really enjoy the mental challenge of what you do?

- What are the tasks you do in your job that you love? Are they transferable to any type of job or unique to what you are now doing? Would you like to do the same on a part-time basis or on a consulting basis where you call the shots on how often and how long each assignment will be?

- Do you have any interest in owning a business? One that speaks to a hobby you have practiced for many years or a franchise in a totally new area of business?

- Would you like to be an employer or an employee, or an independent contractor (self-employed)?

- Is there a field of endeavor you have always wanted to try just for the sheer fun of it, such as woodworker, book seller, or a radio announcer?

Let yourself dream big on this one. One of the key components of a successful third stager is having fun in life. So have fun!

FIND MEANINGFUL ACTIVITY FROM CHILDHOOD

If you are feeling completely lost because you can't identify what it is that would get you out of bed in the morning, try it from another place in the recesses of your mind. I have asked clients to look at the time period between your physical independence from your parents, at around age four to six, and your awareness of adolescence when you had to look, act and be like your peers at age ten to twelve. In that in-between time and place, you did some things that made you want to get out of bed in the summer or run to after school. Something gave you a great sense of accomplishment and you had lots of fun.

From my childhood, I can recall three things: I loved to find discarded piles of finished wood and try to build tree houses in the woods behind our house. I hit the jackpot when I found a neighbor who was renovating the second floor of his house and put piles of wood slats covered with nails and paint stacked neatly at the curb for the garbage truck to pick up the next day. I truly thought I had died and gone to heaven! Picture an eight-year-old dragging all those pieces of wood across an alleyway to a slightly wooded area.

I built the best treehouse ever that week. I raided my father's workshop in the basement for the hammers and all the nails of any size and shape I could find and hurried out to the back to figure out how to work with the tree limbs to place my wood. My mother would call me in for lunch and I couldn't figure out how the time had passed so quickly. The treehouse was, by any other standards, most pathetic, but it didn't matter to me.

Another wonderful activity I loved was to have a neighborhood fair in our backyard. I enlisted the help of my sister and brother and mother to make sure the clotheslines were not "occupied" that day so we could set up "booths" with card tables and bedsheets.

The object was to find stuff in our own homes that other kids would like to have and sell them for pennies. The neighborhood kids would all be assigned a booth, and they could bring whatever they wanted to sell to others that day.

We put up street signs on the telephone poles and passed out fliers to our neighbors to let them know. We even had our lemonade stands on the end of each line. We usually made a grand total of $5 for the day. Many of my friends and their parents grew weary of the upcoming fairs so after a while my pals and I had to look for other ways to pass our time.

But what did I learn from this? From the neighborhood fairs, I learned plenty. I learned that I had skills to enroll and manage people. I learned how to sell. I learned how to take an idea from a thought and put it into reality and I learned to have confidence in my ability to do that. Many of us have ideas that die of loneliness. We never allow ourselves the joy of manifesting the idea into reality because we analyze it to death. Now is the time to start letting your imagination run wild.

From the building of the treehouses, I learned that I can take raw materials and create something that only *I* needed to celebrate. When others looked at my creations, they ridiculed me for the crudeness of it and for the belief I held that it was anything but a collection of old wood. I learned confidence and self-esteem in the face of disbelief and intolerance. I also learned the value of recycling when no one even had a word for it. I had a certain pride in knowing that what one person was willing to send to the trash, I could see endless possibilities in.

Another one of my favorite activities was to build Barbie houses from "stuff" I found in the house. A used spool of thread was the perfect base for the living room table in Barbie's house, and the lid from a jar of olives was the perfect tabletop. Tissues served well as draperies, and chairs and sofas were made of cardboard. Of course, the vibrancy of the interior design was compliments of my most favorite 64-box of Crayola crayons and watercolor paints.

Other than the fact that my brother took great satisfaction in wrecking the whole thing at the end of the day because we wouldn't let him "play" with us, the opportunity to get inventive and be resourceful has served me well in my adult life. It was always a thrill to look at ordinary things in the house and see possibilities in it for the next "room" in the Barbie house. I wondered why I love the section in each *Real Simple* magazine, called Solutions, where they show "new uses for old things." Ahead of my time …

Since long-term memory is still good for most of us, take a stroll down memory lane and try to remember what you wanted to do or who you emulated when you were in that special age group. Did you want to be Elvis Presley? Or an engineer on a train? Or did you fantasize about being a movie star? Did you invent things? Let your mind run.

If you can't remember, call up some of your childhood friends and ask them what they remember about you? What were the things you did together that you all loved? What characteristics did you exhibit that they always remember you for? Were you a leader? Were you the mediator? Were you a troublemaker? Were you the loner? Did you love to read? What books were your favorites when you were a child? If you went to a neighborhood center in the summer, did you love to swim in the pool, play basketball, and play hopscotch or jump rope? Were you in love with the arts and crafts part of the day? Did you go to specific camps? What did you love about being there? Were you a Girl Scout or a Brownie? What badges did you love to earn?

The more you can see the things you loved about your early childhood, the easier it will be to bring those pleasures into your encore stage.

For instance, say you loved to read novels as a kid. You could transfer that love now by getting involved in reading clubs. These clubs assign a book for all to read and then discuss. You can volunteer in the local library to read to children. You can read books and write reviews on the Internet for prospective readers or buyers of the book. You can even be employed as a book reviewer for local newspapers and journals. Maybe you could take a course on writing and actually write a book. The list is endless, but you get the point.

TAKE ANOTHER LOOK
AT RELATIONSHIPS

Another area of success in the encore age is a healthy, supportive relationship with a significant other. How about your relationships? Is it time to move on? Statistically, the second greatest incidence of divorce is now occurring in couples who have been married over twenty-five years.

In this new approach to the encore stage, people are looking at the reasons to stay married. There are those who would argue that human beings are not hard-wired to remain in a single relationship for that long a period of time. And some are beginning to question that personally. If your marriage died emotionally long ago, and you "stayed married for the sake of the children," then maybe it is time to address those long unspoken feelings.

- Does your mate share your enthusiasm for life?
- Does your mate feel that now is the time for leisure and play only?
- Do you now have things to do that you both enjoy, or at least do you give each other the time and space to do the things you enjoy independent of each other? Is he or she jealous of your interests?
- Do you feel boxed in and trapped in the relationship?
- Are you feeling lonely in the relationship? Can your loneliness be resolved by leaving him or her?

Is it something you are looking for outside of yourself? Start looking inward. What is it that would make you happy? If it is another person, you should not blame your significant other. The world of successful encore living encourages you to find that within yourself.

If reading in isolation makes you happy, then take the time to find a quiet spot in your own home or elsewhere (a college library?) to do what you love. If you still have some reason to be together, either for children, grandchildren, or religious reasons, then vow to make your life fulfilled either by being around those you love and admire or by doing things with those who make you feel good.

If you can see that this person you are engaged with is not going to change and you are, it may be time to call it quits. As the old saying goes, when one door closes another one opens. That doesn't mean you will find the man or woman of your dreams, but at least you know what you don't want! And it becomes all the more important to discover what happiness means within you rather than looking for someone to provide it for you.

If you and your mate are very happy and looking forward to what's next, make sure you design a plan that gives you both some freedom and togetherness.

It may also be a time to make new friends. Join a local senior center or senior aerobic group at the Y. Go to events that spark your interests: quilting classes, gardening, skydiving, watercolors, volunteer training, adult learning courses, line dancing, choral groups. Discover those who have decided that retirement does not mean winding down until death comes knocking.

If all your current friends do is discuss their bad news, their failing health, their last three operations, their difficult recovery, their poverty, and their friends who are dying, become less engaged. These people are definite downers. They live in a world of depression, negativity, and confinement. Yes, there are physical limitations we all have and these may even get worse. Yes, there are friends and family who die more often than when we were twenty years old. Yes, there may be money issues for all of us. Yes, there are bad things that happen in this world and maybe even to members of our own families. But it doesn't have to be the focus of your day.

Stories abound of those who have triumphed over physical limitations, emotional scars, and financial deprivation. The more we focus on what unlimited potential we are as human beings, the more we further the human experience for future generations. Focusing on our limitations only holds us back and makes us undesirable to be in anyone's company. Think about it. Do you complain more than you inspire? Resolve to be the latter. See what you can contribute to humanity, not what you can take from it.

SOUL SEARCHING

What about your religious or spiritual affiliation? Does it really speak to your soul or is it something you've just accepted since childhood? Most Boomers ranked very high the need to know more and discover more about their spirituality.

By definition, spirituality has no specific religious affiliation, it is more about a personal connection to God, a higher being, or whatever name you want to give it. It is less about the dogma of an organized religion or a belief in eternal punishment if the rules are not obeyed. It is about questioning the liturgy and protocol we blindly followed in whatever religious training we had as children and young adults.

- How do we find a sense of comfort as the promise of a physical death approaches?

- How do we explain the hardships we now witness as time robs us of our physical capabilities, like sight, taste, smell, and sound?

- Is there something we need to do to be assured our place in eternity like we were told as children? Was that a fairytale to make us sit up straight and be "good"? Or does it have some validity?

- Should I begin to read the Torah, the Bible, the Quran, whatever holy book, more intensely and with a different set of eyes? Will I find answers there for things I never

asked before? What if it is all a hoax? What if there is
no heaven and hell? How do I live a good life? Is that
different than what it was when the holy books were
written?

- Can I find salvation at this late date? Do I need it? Where
  are others who are asking these same questions? Are
  they in my church, my temple, my mosque, a secular
  humanism group or will I find it by being outdoors in the
  peace of the wilderness or at a commune or a retreat?

- Should I abandon what I was taught as a child and look
  elsewhere?

This introspection has never been so powerful as it is now.
Boomers rejoice! This is a good thing. The process of developing
a relationship with a higher being is yours to create. It may take
time. It may come to you in a flash. A personal relationship with
a higher being is yours for the asking. It will take whatever form
you want it to.

With age comes the knowledge that whether you find
spirituality in a pew in a church or in the beauty of the Berkshire
Mountains, or on a ski slope in the Alps, spirituality is present
everywhere. You will need to follow your own compass within
your heart to determine what is right and what is wrong as long as
the laws of our land haven't preempted that choice first.

There are many places to find the truth about this very private
and personal choice. But look to your own self to define it. Others
share your beliefs. If you want to find them, be aware of the clues
you will be given. This is not a clear path for anyone. Try out a few
places and see what speaks to you. Maybe not this one, but maybe
that one. And for some, there is no need to look further than the
religious affiliation you currently have. It speaks to you and so you
find the questions answered there.

In the face of the physical limitations we all do or will
experience, it is a good idea to create a gratitude diary or journal.
If you create a page a day, you will find all the wonderful things
in your life that occurred that day for which you are grateful and

focus on them rather than on what is missing or no longer works as well. Keep your life moving in the direction of that which fills you with joy and wonder, and the things that don't work so well will fade from your sight like those in your rearview mirror.

It is important to look to the future rather than to your past. Forgive yourself for all your past transgressions and know that not one human being will make it to the end of life without their own list of things they wished they had done or not done. But on the other hand, living life with regrets serves no purpose either.

WHAT'S ON YOUR BUCKET LIST?

When most public figures, well into their nineties, are asked if they have any regrets, to a person, they reply, "Not for what I did but in what I failed to do." Like the movie *The Bucket List*, even though the characters didn't achieve everything on their list, they did experience things they would never have done had they not listed those things and set out to do them. Write out your bucket list and get started.

When was the last time you learned something new, a hobby, a skill, or taken a class on some subject you knew nothing about? In a recent article in *Prevention* magazine, German scientists did a study to teach adults aged fifty to sixty-seven to juggle. Though none of them would be hired by a circus, they did learn how to do it. The most significant aspect of this research was the brain scans showed similar changes to those who were learning the same skill in their twenties. The idea of not being able to teach an old dog new tricks is now put to rest.

So get busy and learn something new. For the couch potatoes among us, at least you could exercise your brain by learning a new mental skill such as Sudoku (try some apps on your smartphone) rather than tackling the morning crossword puzzle. And if not Sudoku, then try the *NY Times* crossword rather than the easy ones in the morning paper. Stretch your mind. Reread something that you had to read in high school or college and get to know it from an experienced adult mind. *Great Expectations* is awaiting (happily many classics are free ebook downloads). Most libraries are still open!

Attend a local college offering classes on how to use a computer. (It is really a lot easier than you think.) Check out the senior learning courses for those over the age of sixty or sixty-five. These courses are much shorter in duration but are focused on the intellectual thirst of seniors who would love to know more about almost any topic. They are taught by the faculty of the college who would love to have students in their classrooms who truly want to be there.

The classroom is the perfect place to look for new friends, to establish social connections, and to build a community. Your love of reading, if translated into story hour for children in the libraries, is a way of combining the gift of giving back to the community and the satisfaction of knowing you have contributed in some way to the betterment of the next generation.

Our need for giving back is well documented. The Peace Corps, Doctors without Borders, Medical Missions, Race for the Cure, among many others, are all perfect matches for those of us with a burning desire to give back. There are many websites created to match up people with causes in need of support, both for compensation at an administrative level and in the field, as well as volunteering for no pay.

Depending on your financial situation, you might want to explore the local needs of the community and have a conversation with your United Way office or religious institution. Many nondenominational service agencies are screaming for assistance on many levels. There is no lack of opportunities for any of us to give back.

If you don't know what cause makes you want to jump off the couch and get involved, ask yourself this question: what are the two conditions in this world that I would love to eradicate or solve? Whatever pops up for you needs to be your focus.

A young woman I recently met told me of an experience she had in volunteering in a refugee camp in Haiti. She worked with the orphaned children of AIDS victims and couldn't stop seeing their faces and the anger she felt for the stolen innocence of these real-life children. She was so moved by them that she was seriously considering making it her life's work to be with them and others like them who needed help.

Statistically, the Boomers have had a greater desire to volunteer at clinics and agencies not only in this country but abroad to help make a difference in the world. It would not be unusual to find that somewhere in your heart or mind there is a cause or two with your name on it. Be it a financial contribution or a contribution of your time and energy, there is something you can do to further the collective good of mankind.

Ah, the delicious pleasure of time to play! If not for the boredom of all play and no work makes you an empty person, we all think we would love to do nothing but play when we hit the encore years. But play becomes work when it is all we do. As children, once we got home from school, the promise of play with others was a reward for the "job" of going to school and getting our homework done. And although summers went much too fast, the challenge of a new school year and seeing our friends again soon became our "job" and we took it on—some willingly, some not.

But even as children, we learned that balance was good. Keeping "play" as a big piece of your slice of the successful encore years pie will definitely motivate many people to want to leave the job behind. Play can be combined with several other pie slices to give you leisure that you look forward to.

Golfing is a pastime many Boomers aspire to and one that creates social outlets, friendships, intellectual stimulation, and physical exercise. Big hit on all fronts! Similarly, if you are not a golfer, learning how to golf will also provide definite intellectual stimulation along with all the other attributes of the game. Expand that idea to many other skills and you will have satisfied many of the conditions of a successful encore age.

If not golf, then other physical activities will do. Learn to line dance with or without a partner. Consider sailing, water skiing, snow skiing, or some outdoor sport if you love to be in natural environments. Learn to play bridge, chess, Scrabble, or backgammon if you would prefer to be indoors. Sign up for an exercise class at the local gym, Y, or senior center to keep those muscles strong. If you love water aerobics because it's easier on the bones, give it a try.

Exercise is vital to the well-being of our minds and bodies. It keeps the blood flowing and releases endorphins to the brain, sweetening our outlook on life. So find something to do that you really enjoy for its social as well as its physical benefits.

In short, the encore age is for reexamining the desires we had as children and aligning them with the financial and other resources we have as adults. We now can have the time, the resources, and the freedom to do the things we always wanted to do. Make it the best time of your life.

NO FEAR ABOUT MARRIAGE

He emerged from an online dating service and seemed too good to be true.

My friend who had been married and divorced twice, both bad marriages, thought she found Mr. Wonderful. He treated her unlike her other two husbands. He anticipated her every need. He told her how beautiful she was and how lucky he felt that he found her at this stage in his life. She met his kids, and he met hers. Everybody got along so well.

Cindy opted for the full church wedding. Big white dress, bridesmaids, a reception at the local church hall. He paid for the whole thing. The bride was radiant and smiling, her mother looking fabulous in purple. Her daughters and grandchildren filled the second row of the church. He mouthed the words, "Oh, my God!" when he saw her come down the aisle. It was a beautiful thing.

The honeymoon was the best trip she ever had. They did everything first class. She posted pictures on her Facebook page.

When they got back, they moved into a new five-room apartment he had furnished for her. She started an online business, which had been her dream for years. He was working full-time and life was good.

He told her he got a job in Arizona, a place she had lived before and absolutely loved. It was a dream come true to go with him and be financially stable for once in her life. The movers had been there and the whole apartment was packed.

And then, on the eve of their move west, he was rushed to the hospital with a life-threatening illness. It seems he had had the same illness in the past. But never told her.

The hospital informed her he had no health insurance and his condition required major surgery. They also noted he had previous medical procedures that he had failed to pay for. His medical bills alone were in the neighborhood of $50,000, and this one would add another $20,000. They wanted to know what her decision was.

Oh, and then Cindy found out he had been laid off months ago and had never shared that either. He got up every morning and pretended to go to work, which he never really did. The wedding costs, the honeymoon costs, the furnishings in the apartment were all put on credit cards, which he had no way to repay. The bills were now hers. Over $50,000 in debts she was responsible for.

The move was off, she had nowhere to live, all her furniture was on its way to Arizona. And to add insult to injury, she now had the additional costs to recover her furniture. And then she had to pay for the divorce. And get a job. At age sixty.

Unfortunately this is not fiction. It really happened to one of my dear friends. She apprehensively considered the marriage shortly after she met him. When I asked her if she really loved him, she said he treated her well and she was tired of trying to make it herself. He said all the right things, did all the right things, and she decided to take the risk.

That's one risk that did not pay off.

In the world of finance, we have many types of documented risks when considering an investment: market risk, inflation risk, industry risk, among others. They have more easily quantifiable attributes than emotional risks. Yet, more and more, the emotional risks rule the day.

How do you tell a woman who has struggled for most of her life that the offer of a financially stable, supportive partner might be bad for her? In today's world, it isn't so simple. With the introduction of online dating as a mainstream approach to finding someone to spend your encore years with, finding Mr. (or Ms.) Right does not come without substantial risk.

As my friend Cindy discovered too late.

The use of investigative reports, like credit scores, criminal activity, employment references, and other nosy intrusions, is becoming the norm. It is vital to your own security and that of your loved ones.

Imagine if your children discovered a criminal record for the man who inspired you to love yourself all over again, who took you to places on this planet you only wished you could visit, who wined you and dined you on a seemingly unending source of money? To find out he was a fraud would be too painful, emotionally, financially, psychologically, and socially.

We can all recount the stories of Baby Boomer friends who met someone through a church event, a trip overseas, or as a part of the many travel agency–produced adventures. They never thought they could feel that way again. That giddy romantic feeling, the desire to spend every waking hour with him, and the next big steps: formal dating, meeting the families, talk of moving in together. And for some, this was the most wonderful thing in their lives. A new lease on life.

Yet thousands of women are duped every year in this country by those who prey on widows, divorced women, and women who have the outward appearance of having some financial security. It has become a new way of making a living for many men on the online dating scene.

The old-fashioned way of meeting someone with whom you share a common interest, or because someone, who is family or friend, knows of a likely partner for you still makes the safest way to find that special someone. That common connection makes it harder to be a scammer if you are accountable to too many others, especially if the one who introduced you works with a friend or family member.

Where does that leave us as far as the formality and legality of marriage is concerned?

Somewhere in the middle.

It seems somewhat silly to choose your marital status based on your income sources, but that is the decision many Boomers are forced to make.

If you are on Social Security under your own earnings history, then it would not mean any change in that aspect of your income. If you are collecting benefits under a former spouse's insurance, or as a widow, it might mean a full or partial loss of income if you remarry, depending on your age when you remarry. Best to check the current laws before you get hitched.

Given all the financial impacts of marrying in the encore stage, many couples are forgoing the trip to the altar in favor of having a better standard of living without compromising their income streams. They might decide to pool their resources to improve their lifestyles but hopefully not without some written, legal agreement that will demonstrate the intended dissolution of that agreement when either dies.

It allows for the marital benefits of "two can live cheaper than one" without the disadvantages of divorce. Some, however, feel the moral issues of living together without benefit of the marriage certificate outweighs the financial aspects. It depends on where you land on this touchy issue.

Certainly, my friend who was buffaloed into believing her life would be better with the ring, found her life severely compromised by the same. In her case, her religious beliefs prevented her from living with him. So she paid a dear price.

Ellen was a woman with a college degree in a specialized field. She will never be without work. Her skills will always be in demand in the medical area. She married a young man whom she described as a starving artist. He was quite a maverick and prone to fits of temper. Ellen assumed it was part of the territory, the temperamental artiste. After living with his sullen disposition and general malaise for over a decade, she decided there must be something more to life than this. Having no children to concern herself with (other than her husband, she would note), she divorced the artist and set out to find another man.

She registered with three online dating services, carefully vetting each in many different areas: for success rates (defined as the number of resulting marriages), for the occurrence of married people posing as single people, for initiation and ongoing costs, for online security of personal data, and other measures.

She learned the ins and outs of the system and what catch phrases to look for, always opting to meet a prospect in a public place, and all the other tried-and-true navigation devices.

She met and dated several men over a period of two years until she found one she really liked. She just liked him; she didn't fall madly in love with him. She was caught between a former lover who had recently become available and a man who had treated her very well and was madly in love with her. She had strong feelings for the former and was intrigued by the latter.

She opted for the latter.

He proposed to her in Paris on her birthday, had a wedding of simple but classy taste, bought a home in a tony section of the area, and they have had a wonderful, rewarding life. He is successful, adventurous, sociable, happy, and most of all, not a starving artist.

Ellen played this one well. She had a credit check done on him, police reports, full medical report and satisfied herself that she would not be walking into a mine field. She did her homework. She offered him the same security reporting on her life, which he really appreciated. Both of them had been married previously, and neither one of them wanted to take on the other's baggage.

It's nice when it works out that way.

Ellen wanted the financial security of a marriage but also realized the trauma of divorce. She had a prenuptial agreement signed as a stipulation to getting married. He wanted the same. Although this is a tough conversation to have and will test the strength of the couple, it is a necessary evil in today's society. It puts a little more skin in the game when the first urge to split comes along.

Mom never had that kind of agreement when she married my dad. It was always assumed the "for better or worse" part was taken seriously because, really, where would she go if a divorce happened. She had no formal education, would have no status in the world as a divorced woman, no church would accept her, and she would face the wrath of her friends and family. If they divorced, the assumption was that she was not taking care of her husband properly and the fault was surely hers.

Thankfully, that is not the case now.

So if you are divorced, how do you move on to the next phase of your life?

There are no rules. You kind of make them up as you go along. The jump to get back in the dating scene is fraught with peril and potential disease. There are those who believe it is imperative to have a medical test done before you entertain sexual relations with a new significant other. Or for a casual one-night stand. (Don't give me that look!)

If you choose to stay uncommitted to anyone, then your financial situation is easy to manage. It's about you and you. Your money pots will generally stay the same.

If you choose to be in a committed relationship but reside in your own abodes, then the same is true except when it comes to activities you both enjoy. Who pays for dinner when you both dine out? Who pays for accommodations and activity fees when you travel? Do you share the cost of gasoline and tolls when you travel?

Again, there are no rules.

Recently a woman who blogs wrote about the idea of sharing all the expenses. Sounds good in principle, but tough to manage. If one pays with a credit card and the other pays in cash, does the one who pays on the credit card get the rewards points? Yes. How does that equal out when you plan a trip?

If not equal, then do you divvy it up by income level? If he makes less than you do, do you risk offending his masculinity by offering to pay more than half? Would he be offended if you offered to pay anything toward the tab? How will you know until after you see who picks up the bill?

If this develops into a more committed relationship where you move in together, you will need to put more thought into this. If one earns more than the other, then does that person pay a higher percentage of the fixed costs such as rent/mortgage, utilities, taxes, and anything else? If you are a bigger eater than he, do you pay more for food? Who owns the toys, like the flat screen TV, the microwave? Who owns the collections? The dogs and cats?

Every one of these questions poses a ton of issues that will ring all your bells in regard to your deep-seated beliefs relative to money and control. Best be aware of them and have these conversations before you are too far gone in the arrangements and can't get out.

If you choose to stay single while living together and plan on children (or not plan!), then it gets even stickier. Whose name does the child take? Do you have custody established? Who is responsible for child support? Medical costs? Education costs? Clothing costs? Food costs?

It is often at this point that couples marry. It's easier to manage the addition of a human being in a marriage than not. Of course, if you are marrying for a second or third time after age fifty, you will probably not be concerned about child-bearing issues. Or maybe you will.

I have a friend who spent most of her adult life pursuing a doctoral degree. She found herself in a unique position of taking over a department that had been run by a legend who made one fatal mistake. In doing so, it opened the doors for her to be the most logical choice to run the department.

Around that same time, her parents became ill. She had just moved into an apartment about twenty-five minutes away when the first of them came down with cancer. Rather than move back in with them, she spent most of her days and nights taking care of them and rarely spending time at home.

On one such day when she made a brief appearance at home to take her garbage out, she met her next-door neighbor. He was a sweet, shy guy, about ten years her junior. He told her he would be happy to care for her apartment by taking out the garbage and walking and feeding her dog while she cared for her parents. Taken by his kindness, she soon discovered he was a transplant to the area and knew nothing about where to dine, shop, or have fun. On the days she was home for dinner, she cooked some meals for him and showed him around the area.

They soon became an item.

She had long given up on finding anyone to be involved with because of her demanding academic schedule and her caretaking role. She was amazed at what had shown up in her life when she least expected it.

After a few months of falling in love and introducing each other to their parents, she said, "It's silly to keep two apartments when we live in one. So when the lease is up on mine, we'll move in together."

And then they decided to get married. Both Mom and Dad were at the wedding and were delighted to see their baby girl so happy. Shortly after they bought a home together, Mom and Dad both passed away within a year of each other. She decided it was "time for me and my husband. I spent so much time on everyone else's needs, now it's time for us."

One big change was to adopt a baby. What a change! At age fifty, she realized trying to bring a pregnancy to term was risky both for her and for a baby. But the urge to parent was there for both of them. In another time, it would have been deemed insane for a woman and a man of that age to adopt.

And the rules continue to be broken.

Despite the fact that the societal norms are being forced to move with the tide, the financial rules have not moved that much. Still foremost in the rule book is to make sure you protect yourself and your assets.

It is never a stupid idea to take inventory of what you have before you make any kind of commitment to another person and know what you are willing to give up to have it. That sacrifice may be for the good in the long run, but in the short term, before you know whom you are hitching your wagon to, caution is the order of the day.

If you are widowed or divorced and have children, independent or not, consider the following:

- How do you want to title the property you own, or will own, with another? Property owned as joint tenants with right of survivorship has different legal consequences than joint tenants with the entireties. Both of these are valid ways to title properties but each has drawbacks and advantages. Understand these before you agree to sign the deed(s). June didn't realize her late husband owned their house in joint name with his children after his first wife died. "I thought he redid his will after we got married and now I have no home to call my own."

- If you predecease your significant other (SO), will some or all of your personal assets go to your SO or your children? Will you split them among all parties? Does your SO know that? Martha thought her new husband's house would automatically go to her when he passed. She then discovered her stepchildren were now her landlord and wanted to sell the house to get their inheritance. "Don't I have any rights as his wife?" she asked. The answer is no, if he signed a will saying it was to be theirs. She got a life insurance policy and some investments, but not the house.

- Are all your checking and savings accounts in joint name? If so, you will have access to them once your husband or SO passes if both your names are on the checks. If they are set up with only one signature required to sign a check, then you are good; if it requires both to be valid, you have a problem. Best to have checking accounts in individual names so each of you has immediate access to cash when needed. Rachel knew her SO was the bill payer in the family but didn't realize the checking account had only his name on it. When she tried to access the checking account, the teller told her she could not withdraw the funds. "How do I get money from this account if he is out of town?" The answer was she could not. She opened her own checking account on the spot.

- If you are the key breadwinner of the family, will your employee benefits be available to your SO if you died? Some companies do not recognize unmarried couples as having spousal rights. So even if you named your SO as your beneficiary of some group life insurance or retirement plans, your plan administrator may throw up some flak if your SO tries to claim the benefits. John lived with Sally for over fifteen years. Everyone thought they were married especially when they moved to another city for Sally to take the job. Her boss knew they were not married and wondered if she knew the employee handbook specifically mentioned the absence of benefits for unmarried employees. "I never knew I was not providing for John because of the handbook rules. And I don't know if that is legal. Should I press it and risk the possibility of losing my job?" Sally wondered.

- If you bring some considerable assets to a successive marriage, will the terms of your estate documents automatically assume it all goes to your husband if you predecease him? Not always what you want to have happen. Consider the possibility that your husband develops some mental or physical infirmity and will need nursing home care. If you die before he does, all your assets might go to the nursing home and none to your children or family. Marilyn thought it was the loving thing to do to care for her husband by pooling their assets to care for his disability. What she did not know is by doing the "right thing" she was guaranteeing the complete evaporation of all their assets. Getting some specific legal advice to protect some of it from medical costs would have saved her something to live on. "What I didn't understand, until it was too late, is that I am entitled to preserve some assets to allow me to maintain my standard of living while George was taken care of by government programs he was entitled to."

- If your children are married and later survive a divorce, do you have your legal documents set up to specifically disinherit your children's former spouse(s) and name your children and/or grandchildren as your beneficiaries? If you name your daughter-in-law or son-in-law specifically by name and not by relationship to you, it is possible they could contest a will you created to give them a part of your estate. I'm not saying it is always successful, but it will cause emotional trauma and hatred at a time your children may be grieving your loss. Best to have language in your will expressly naming them as current spouses to your children and only in that relationship will they inherit any of your assets, if you want them to. Mary and her late husband had started a gifting program where they gave each of their three daughters and sons-in-law the maximum they could give each year. As of this writing, the amount was $13,000 or a total of $26,000 per year to each couple. When Mary's husband died, she wanted her daughters and sons-in-law to continue to receive that annual gift, but one of her daughters, Anne, was divorcing and did not want to include her estranged husband in that gift. Mary was approached by her estranged son-in-law to give him his $13,000 as she had in the past. She consulted a lawyer and he told her she was under no obligation to give the money to her son-in-law. Her daughter was furious that she even considered it. "I

only wanted to do what was right for both of them and
I hated being put in the middle of it all. I knew he was
unemployed and really needed the money. After all, he
is the father of my grandchildren and I have nothing
against him."

- As I wrote earlier, there are no rules about living together
  unmarried, including the laws addressing or more likely
  not addressing the issues of same-sex cohabitation.
  Essentially they are the same as opposite-sex cohabitation.
  The only relief you have is to sit with an attorney and
  put in writing all the legal direction you can for your
  surviving partner and for your respective families.

In a few years, this "no rules" about co-habitating will probably
disappear as the desire for people to live their lives without the
legal status of marriage becomes more and more the situation
of choice. Notwithstanding the religious imperatives, we have
reached the point in our society that more parents of newborn
babies are not married at the time of their child's birth than are
married. It's a trend that has doubled in the last twenty years.

Janet, a retired teacher, met a guy through a friend at her
church Sunday School. Jake was a very handsome widower who
had enjoyed a great relationship with his recently deceased wife
and was having a difficult time being social without her. Janet,
never married, felt a strong sense of compassion and empathy
with Jake. She realized several other women in her church group
felt the same. She was embarrassed by this feeling of jealousy
whenever any of these other women engaged Jake in conversation.

Why do I have any claim on him? she wondered to herself. It
reminded her of all the times as a young girl in college she felt she
was the one left standing against the wall when the young men
came over to ask the young women to dance. No confidence in
herself as a "contender."

Then a thought struck her. Why would I let the feelings of
a twenty-year-old dictate who I am as a fifty-eight-year-old? She
mustered up her strength and went over to Jake at the end of their

next Sunday School meeting at the social hour and asked him if he would like to join her next week at the dine-around. This was a social event designed to encourage all singles to meet at a member's house with the only requirement that they bring a bottle of wine or a dessert.

He readily accepted and looked forward to the time together with her. He thanked her for the invitation and then called her a few days later to join him for coffee after a day at his golf club. She felt great that she had initiated it, had arranged their first meeting in a public place, and would get to know him in the security of a friend's house. I don't know how it all turned out, but it meant a lot to her to get herself out of her rut. I suspect it did well for him too.

ACTION STEPS

1. If you are single and in an unmarried relationship, make time to talk to your significant other about what you would both like to happen to your assets when either of you dies.

2. If you are single and not in a relationship, consider your intentions with your personal assets, especially if you have no living heirs. Would you like to fund a scholarship at your alma mater, or do you have a favorite cause you would like to support? Get this on a notarized piece of paper with witnesses.

3. If you are in a committed relationship, please discuss with your partner what living arrangements you would expect from each other if you are the owner of your house in which he or she is currently living.

4. There are many counselors, religious and non, who can give you some guidance on the desirability of being single or married. You may find at your encore stage in life, the idea of being single is a status worth keeping.

NO FEAR ABOUT BEING A WIDOW

As I write this chapter, my mother has experienced for the second time in her life the physical, emotional, and financial upheaval of being a widow. My stepfather passed away after a three-year battle with bladder cancer, and we all observed the slow deterioration of his body, his mobility, and his spirit. After a short stay in hospice, the end finally came.

True to his nature, he told her she would be fine financially and did have the presence of mind when he was first diagnosed with the disease to "get his financial house in order." He was a quiet and private man. He told her little about the particulars but enough that she knew what major assets were involved. He even went so far as to write on a small 3x5 piece of paper what income sources she would have and what assets he knew she would inherit.

Many women were not privileged to share in the level of communication that existed between my mother and my stepfather. To some men, especially those of the Greatest Generation (post–World War II), they believed that their wives should find out what they would have (or what they would owe!) after their husband's death, putting them in a situation wondering if they were dealt the winning lottery ticket or if they would be doomed to a life of penury. Their wives were caught in a financial maelstrom at a time when their emotional world was in shambles as well.

The perpetuation of our cultural norm was the reason for this: most men did not want their wives to know what they had simply because it was not in the purview of women to know these things or for fear they, or their families-in-law, would spend it or because their wives simply did not want to be bothered with such things.

As was the custom, there were clearly defined roles within a marriage, and the management of personal finances, beyond the paying of household bills, was not in the job description of the wife. This lack of information and awareness of what to do with the money they might inherit was left to their sons, if they had them, or to the "trusted advisor" formerly used by their husbands (undoubtedly another man).

But being a widow adds an emotional dimension to this lack of knowledge at a time when its absence is most acutely felt. A woman's financial security, her place of residence, her ability to function in the same social circles, her lifestyle in general may be diminished if not ended at the same time she aches for the emotional support and care her husband provided. It's a double whammy.

There is the initial trauma of deciding on burial arrangements, services to be conducted and by whom, what special tributes your late husband would have liked for the ceremony, the selection of pallbearers, the burial site, and the dinner afterward. But it all pales in comparison to the stark reality of being alone. After all the well-wishers' promises of unlimited support and help cease, and the generous donations of food run out, the big questions loom: What do I do with each day?

- Should I stay here?

- Should I sell my home and go somewhere else?

- Will I miss my friends?

- At this stage in my life, do I want to make new friends?

- Should I live closer to my children?

- Is it too soon to be making these decisions?

In a word, yes. Too many times, I have seen clients who reacted to demands by their well-intentioned in-laws and children to leave the house, sell it, and move somewhere else. And it failed miserably.

My advice to women who are recently widowed is to make no decisions about your living arrangements until at least six months after the death of your husband—preferably, a year. By then, you can be thinking more clearly, your financial condition will be stabilized, and your desire to move or not to move will be rational, not reactionary.

I have offended many children of these widowed clients who all wanted different things for Mom, and all were sure they had the right answer. I, of course, was not legally able to demand that Mom spend the time mourning her loss and getting her head clearer, and at times, I failed to stem the tide that carried Mom to the homes of her well-meaning children.

But invariably, the reactionary life choices are usually regretted; a reasoned plan of action is always appreciated and has a greater chance of succeeding.

HONEY, WHERE IS OUR MONEY?

Start now to find out what your financial life looks like. This, of course, assumes a willingness of your spouse to participate, but even if he does not, here are some ways you can find out what assets and income you both own. So rather than be a victim of this life-altering event, you could gently approach this topic without setting off alarms in your husband's head.

I have often advocated having this type of serious conversation in a neutral setting in which you have created a sense of calm and trust, such as an anniversary celebration, a Valentine's Day dinner, New Year's Day, a weekend away or a vacation trip. Certainly not one where the children and other members of the family are present.

Begin the conversation talking about your fears of having to go through life alone without him and then ask him if he thinks you would be able to live comfortably if he was the one to go first. After his initial shock and unspoken concerns that you are planning his demise, and reassurances from you that you are not, he may begin to open up.

A simple, "You'll be fine," doesn't cut it.

You might further ask if there is something written somewhere that would outline where your assets are, like what brokerage house or financial planner you use (if you haven't been included in the relationship, now would be a good time to start by requesting a meeting with him or her, but more on that later), where we keep our wills and other documents, like marriage license, his military discharge papers, your Social Security cards, for example. If important documents are kept somewhere in the house, ask him to show you where.

You can couch these inquiries by relating all of this to a friend who recently was widowed and the difficult time she had in finding all this. And because you know he loves you, you would like to be spared that pain at a time that would already be filled with trauma. Or something like that. You know your old man better than anyone, so use this as a guide. *But please ask.* When he's gone, it's too late and you will have to imagine or guess where he kept things.

To press on, if you get this far, consider asking him to introduce you to your attorney, your insurance agent, your broker/ financial planner, your accountant, and your banker if there is one, especially if your husband owns a business. And position it that way intentionally, using "our" professional advisors, rather than "his."

You need not make these introductory dinners anything more than a social event, but use your gut instinct to judge the professional's character and the willingness of that person to include you as an equal and not as an accessory to your husband. It will serve you well to know those people before you need them. If you do not trust these people or find you dislike their attitude toward you, make a mental note to begin to look elsewhere on your own to create social relationships with other professionals you would like to deal with in the future.

At the very least you should know the answers to the following questions:

- Do we have a will? Is it in the attorney's office with a copy in our lock box at home? Who is our attorney?

- What insurance policies do we have? Which ones name me as the owner and/or beneficiary? Where are the policies? Who is the agent? What is the payoff amount?

- Where are our investments? Do you have an investment plan through the business? Who is the contact person at the office? Who are our brokers? Do you want me to continue to use them when you're gone?

- Does the business give you a "deferred compensation plan" (an agreement to pay part of his deferred salary to him for a period after he retires or dies)? Where is the paperwork that explains that? Who is the person at the office who would know of this?

- What bank has the mortgage on our house(s)? Is there insurance to pay off those mortgages when you die? Or if I predecease you? Where is that insurance policy?

- Do we use a financial planner? If so, who is that person? How can I reach him or her?

- Did you set aside a pot of money, not invested anywhere, that I can use to tide me over until life insurance money is paid out to me? If so, where is that money, what bank account? How did you determine how much to set aside?

- Do we have any college funds for our children/ grandchildren? If so, where are they and how can I access them if you die before they finish college?

- Do you have a living will? Am I named as your representative? If so, under what circumstance am I to tell them to use no heroic measures to keep you alive?

- Should I have a similar document? Where is this document? Is it your intention to be an organ donor?

- If you have online access to our accounts, what are the user names and passwords I need to have access to them?

- Where are all the bank accounts? Anything offshore? How do I access those?

- Is there a safe deposit box at a bank? How do I access that? What's in it? Where is the key?

- Do you have a prepaid burial or funeral plan?

Once you have all that information, consider yourself good to go. And be sure to set up a time each year when you sit down and review that information. At this point, you do not need to understand all of it, but just know where those papers are and what they mean.

BASICS ABOUT ASSETS

Beyond that, there are at least three fundamental financial concepts you should know and that I explain in detail next:

1.   Titling of assets
2.   An emergency fund
3.   An inventory of what assets you each own

In titling the assets, let's start with a primer on what the different options mean.

- *Jointly-held* means that you and another person are equal owners of an asset. It means that at the death of either party, the other survivor has full and equal rights to the use of the asset (house, car) and that right becomes immediately available at death. Should you predecease your husband, that joint asset goes directly to him.

- This type of joint ownership between a husband and a wife is usually referred to as *tenants by the entirety*, a form unique to married couples. You might notice on a monthly statement from an investment company the title of your account will have both names listed and the initials JTWROS after it. This stands for "Joint Tenants with Rights of Survivorship" and lets you know that you have 100 percent access to this account, as does your husband.

- In *community property* states, the assumption is that you own half of everything you have in the marriage including real estate property. And he owns half of everything you own as well.

How will you know if you live in a community property state? Well, there are nine states in the U.S. that are community property states: Arizona, California, Idaho, Louisiana, Nevada, New Mexico, Texas, Washington, and Wisconsin. One of our territories, Puerto Rico, and the state of Alaska give you the option to have your property owned as community property and several Native American lands do too.

Why would you want to own most everything in joint names? There are really good reasons to do so, but more importantly, there are some disadvantages as well. Owning property in joint names, such as your house, vacation homes, and most real estate, means that if your husband dies, these pieces of property are yours to do with what you will. It also means you do not have to look for a place to live and you do not have to sell the house, the vacation home or any piece of property until you are ready to do so. That, of course, assumes your home is either fully paid for or you have the income to continue to pay the mortgage(s) and to pay the household expenses of maintaining the property. If you can afford to stay in the home, that is one fewer issue to have to address in the first few months of widowhood.

Another form of joint ownership that is helpful for this transition is to own at least one checking account in joint names. And the titling of this account should read "John OR Jane Smith."

That allows either of you to write checks and pay bills. That will also buy you some time until you determine where you will live. The cable company doesn't care if your husband dies; they still want the monthly payment. Same with the electric company and the phone company. You get the idea.

If your husband paid the bills from his checking account and your name is not on the checking account, then legally you have no way to pay the bills using his checks until any life insurance money or your own funds are used to do that. Many women do not carry enough money in their own accounts (if they even have them) to pay all their living expenses for a few months.

If your husband was computer savvy, he may have had many of the bills automatically deducted from his checking account. Without knowing his user names, passwords, and websites where he paid the bills, there is no way for you to keep track of what bills need to be paid or when they are due. If the money runs out in his checking account, you may not be able to avoid disconnections on your cable, phone, gas, electricity or other utilities until you get a notice from them in the mail. If he set it up so that all communications were sent electronically via email, then you must know the user name and password to get into his email account too.

Now the second—maybe the most important—tool you should have in your toolbox is an emergency account. This checking account, which should be titled with the word "or" in the names on the account, should maintain an amount equal to at least three months of normal living expenses.

This account needs to be easily accessible by either writing a check or making a withdrawal at the bank to provide immediate cash to the widow to pay for final expenses such as funeral costs, medical bills, transfer costs for the change of property to your name, and legal costs, if any. This account will be your lifeline until assets held in your husband's name, life insurance claims, and any other employee benefits become available. That process with all the paperwork and required copies of death certificates will take at least a few months to be completed.

This emergency account is a MUST for all women. If a debilitating accident or sickness happens to your husband, you may need to access this fund until disability benefits or paychecks come in.

So besides owning everything in joint names, what else is there? You should keep some money in an account *in your own name.* This account could be a regular checking account (make sure you can keep the minimum balance so you don't get hit with monthly fees), and/or an interest-bearing checking/money market account, which usually requires a minimum balance of about $1,000, or a money market fund, an account held by an investment company that pays interest as well.

These last two money market accounts/funds often limit the number of checks you can write on those accounts to five a month. These accounts should be for your own spending: gifts to children or grandchildren, a trip to the hair salon, buying your own clothes, for example. In all fairness, this account should be mirrored by one for your husband. This allows for some freedom and some real education on how to keep track of the money you spend and the way you spend it. It is with this solo account that you might try to create a budget for yourself and learn to save some of it.

Having your own money could lead to an opportunity to begin an investment program for yourself in your own name. Most women are unfamiliar with the language of the investment world and would be well served by starting or joining an investment club. This is a wonderful medium to learn about investments and to bring a group of like-minded women together to learn. There is plenty of information on the Internet to tell you how to get one started and how to find friends to join. This is not a Money Circle that I have been describing, although it may be an outgrowth of a money club.

Now, on the flip side of things, establishing credit in your own name is something most Boomer women fail to do. If all your credit was in jointly-named accounts and your husband dies, the availability of future credit dies with him. I know of a woman who recently checked with her insurance company as to why her premiums were getting so high year after year. She wondered why she didn't see the "longevity discount" on the premium notice.

The representative told her that the discount is only available for those who have been with the company over ten years. She informed the rep that she and her husband had been with that company for over thirty years. The rep told her that the account was in joint names for twenty-five of those thirty years and her history with the company only counts from the day the policy was taken out in her name alone. She said she is not done fighting this one yet, but here's to her determination!

Another widowed woman, Rachel, with a net worth of over $10 million and her friend, Elise, who was a married schoolteacher for over forty years, were on vacation in Europe. This was before the Euro was the common currency in Europe and they found that they needed to get French francs (cash) for an excursion on the railways of France. When they presented their credit cards, the millionairess's card was rejected.

The credit card account was in her late husband's name and she rarely, if ever, used the credit card because she always paid in cash. On this one instance when she needed to use a credit card, the credit was denied because it was not in her name. Elise laughingly chided her friend who said this would be a first in her life: her personal finances were nowhere as good as her friend's but her credit was better.

So if you are not a working woman, and have credit established in your husband's name, as Mrs. John Doe, you should get a credit card with your name on it from a local department store where you regularly shop.

If you use your husband's first name (John, for example), then have the credit card issued in the name of Jane Doe. Use the card for making purchases and then pay off the balance if you can each month. If not, then make a payment greater than the minimum each month to show your "good credit."

Then start with another card, such as American Express, which is not specific to a region or a store. Or a gasoline credit card. That will enhance your personal credit and will allow you to have access to credit if your husband dies before you do. And use them to the extent you can afford to repay them.

Once you get the card, it does not mean that the card issuer will continue to keep the card active. The tiny print in the agreement says that an inactive card will become invalid after a certain period of inactivity. Don't let that happen. Even if you use it once a year to buy $20 worth of something, do so. Your ability to rely on credit may be the saving grace that keeps you going until your financial situation in early widowhood is more stable.

SAVVY WAYS TO FIND THE SECRET STASH

Now undoubtedly, the most difficult of the three basic steps is getting an inventory of the assets you both own and in whose name they are held. As mentioned earlier, this is a ticklish subject for many men to engage in. But some manipulative and perhaps underhanded methods of doing so will yield good results.

Those who have filled in the infamous FAFSA forms for college education loans and other funding know that you must disclose all your assets and income on this form. If you have children who are attending or did attend college in the last decade you might have a built-in solution to this problem with little or no resistance. Make sure you look closely at the disclosures on that form to find out what information you can as to what you own and in whose name the other assets are owned.

Your income taxes will also give you the names of the financial institutions that hold accounts in either your or your husband's names. They can be found on Schedule B of the tax return. Look for those statements that match the company names on the tax return and see if you can find as many accounts as are listed on that page.

Also, on the front page of the income tax return (Form 1040) are references to income from other sources, some of which are separate schedules included in the tax return, such as Schedule C and Schedule E. These schedules show sources of income from partnerships, real estate investments, and other business ventures, which you may not know your husband is invested in. These would help you get an idea of what activities he is involved with and what potential income or investments you can work with in the future.

You have the right to examine every tax return every year before you sign it. I would suggest you become more familiar with your returns in the future. Not to be adversarial with him, but to allow it to be a launching point for a more involved conversation in the near future.

And if you recently refinanced a piece of property you owned, the disclosure forms for that process require full details of what is owned and by whom, including copies of the most recent statements to support the numbers put on the form. This would be a treasure trove of information for you. This would also be a good point of reference to begin a discussion of your personal finances if you asked about what new interest rate you got on your refinancing. The fact that you asked might give your husband some indication that you are interested in knowing about your personal finances.

In many ways, men would appreciate sharing the burden of the financial security for your family. An expression of your concern and interest would go a long way in making him feel that some of the pressure is off if he thought you were a partner in the process rather than a dependent. But remember, the cultural norm is that he should have the sole responsibility for this, and it is his duty to provide. If you approach this task with a willingness to help in making it work rather than as an inquisition into his failings, you have a chance at making your marriage a true partnership. How you approach this is key to its success.

BUSINESS AFTER BURIAL

Should the grim reaper take him first, then what do you do and in what order?

After the initial burial or cremation arrangements are made, the ceremony in celebration of his life is an important part of the grieving process. I will make the assumption that the ceremony would be one of honoring the deceased but I have heard of some rather unusual wakes.

A woman who detested the man she was married to for over fifty years wore the traditional black to the church and to the cemetery, but when they came back to the parish center for the after-burial dinner, she announced quite loudly that she was glad to be rid of the SOB and promptly stripped back the black jacket to reveal a bright red shirt. She announced that she had achieved her goal to outlive him, God willing, so she could learn what life was like in freedom from her dear departed husband. She is still living a good ten years (post age ninety!) after his death and now wishes that "God would take her."

So, assuming you would not be relieved and happy to see him go, let's take a look at what needs to be done and in what order. The first order of business is to get at least ten copies of his death certificate from the funeral director or the person who was responsible for handling his bodily remains. Once you have these in hand, then you need to make some phone calls to the people who hold the assets you will inherit.

Where should you begin to get the work-related benefits to which you are entitled? Start with the human resources department or the supervisor for whom your husband worked. If they are unaware of his passing, make sure you let them know his date of death. Often, if he was already retired, pension payments may be rescinded if a check was paid to him at the beginning of the month in which he died. Or they may require a partial repayment for the days in the month he did not survive.

Assuming your husband had some advice at the time he selected his beneficiary for his pension benefit, he undoubtedly made arrangements for you to have some portion of that benefit paid to you for your lifetime.

The paperwork to initiate that will require a copy of his death certificate and a form to be completed. That process will take about a month or less to complete. Choose an automatic monthly deposit of your benefit into your checking account. That saves time and mailing costs, is a far more secure form of payment, and is a written record of the transaction.

If your husband was a highly paid executive or the owner of the firm, there may be a form of deferred compensation in place too. As mentioned earlier, this is a benefit given to those whose income is at or near the highest income tax bracket. It was designed as a way to *defer* some portion of current earned income to sometime in the future when his tax bracket was presumably less, like at retirement. So the amount of money in this plan can be substantial and is usually payable to a surviving spouse if the employee did not take the money or while taking it, he had a remaining balance to be paid out. This could be a major benefit for you if it exists. The people who would know of this are most likely those in the human resources department, the controller of the company, or their accountant, usually a CPA. There is also paperwork to support that plan, which you may be aware of, but the absence of it does not prevent you from asking about the plan or from receiving the benefits of it.

Another form of deferred compensation is the stock option plan. Without getting too detailed, the stock option plans are an incentive given by the employer to key employees to reward their contributions to the growth of their company. These plans have a definite time period from the date when they were issued to the date they expire, usually ten years. The employee (your husband) has (or had) the right to buy the stock of his employer's company at a specific price anytime during these ten years. That price was determined by the value of the stock at the time the stock option plan was issued (say, $25 per share in 2005).

Normally, there is no desire to buy the stock at the price it is offered by the stock option plan if the stock is selling on the stock exchange for less than that. If the reverse is true, for example, the price to buy on the stock exchange is around $30, and he buys the stock from the company at the lower price ($25 per share), the difference between the price he buys it from the plan ($25) and the price it is selling for ($30 per share) is considered to be compensation to him and is taxable income to him.

Since each stock option usually lasts for about ten years, if your husband dies before he has exercised all the options he was entitled to, you may be permitted to do so for a period of one or two years after his death. If you do not do so, the options will automatically expire and no financial transactions will have been deemed to happen. Of course, if the exercise price of the option is greater than the price it is selling for on the stock exchange, the option has no value and will most likely expire on its own. This could be a huge bonus of income to you if you work with an advisor to help you determine whether or not the stock option plan has some value. See the following example.

STOCK OPTION EXAMPLE

Year	2005	2006	2007	2008	2009	2010	2011	2012	2013	2014
Stock Price	$25	$26	$28	$30	$35	$32	$28	$30	$35	$34
Option Price	$25	$25	$25	$25	$25	$25	$25	$25	$25	$25
+/-	$ -	$1	$3	$5	$10	$7	$3	$5	$10	$9

There may be life insurance benefits paid by the company to a beneficiary. Ask about that too. If the cause of his death was due to some incident relative to a work-related fatal injury, you may have double indemnity, or twice the amount of the death benefit, not to mention a potential lawsuit to reclaim your financial loss due to his death. Under no circumstances should you sign off on any legal documents offered by the employer or the employer's attorney relinquishing your rights to sue by accepting the check for the life insurance offered by the employer. Find your own lawyer to review it first.

For most employees, and especially for those who were of the senior executive level, the group life insurance benefits can be substantial. Employees are often granted at least one times salary as a death benefit, but those in the corner offices can often get up to five times their base salary in life insurance benefits. This could be the single most significant benefit you receive from your husband's company.

One note of caution here: often the life insurance company who offered the insurance plan to your husband's employer will offer the "assistance" of one of their representatives to call on you to explain the many ways you can take the benefits. There are income options that will guarantee a payment to you for life and something leftover for your heirs, the purchase of an annuity, which will allow you to have a lifetime income benefit or a vehicle to pass it to the next generation, or the option to take it in a lump sum "safely" placed in a money market fund with the insurance company with check-writing privileges.

DO NOT TAKE ANY OTHER OPTION BUT THE LUMP SUM.

All the rest are designed to leave money with the company for them to invest elsewhere or to generate new commission income for one of their agents. If you work with a financial planner, his or her knowledge of investing your money should allow you unlimited freedom to access the money and to generate a lifetime of income.

Then you must realize that you will be able to file your tax returns as a joint return with your deceased husband for the last year in which he was alive. That means you must work with your CPA or your own accountant (please, not a national franchise for this important tax year) to prepare the return.

There are many important tax deductions available to a jointly filed return that should not be missed. And unless you remarry, this benefit is helpful to your tax status with the IRS, meaning you will pay less as a married couple than as a single person.

Work with your accountant as soon as possible in the first quarter of the year following your husband's death to make sure that you have the necessary paperwork to allow the CPA to properly prepare your return. He or she will most likely request a copy of your previous year's return to compare notes.

As discussed earlier, there are many important pieces of information contained on a tax return that are like clues to a detective, if you know how to interpret them. The tax return will alert your CPA to investments and employee benefits that will require some tax documents to complete your return. If you can't find them, it is easier to start requesting them early in the year rather than on April 14, the day before your tax return needs to be filed.

Perhaps the easiest and most readily available income comes not from any work-related benefits, but from Uncle Sam—Social Security benefits. If your husband was already receiving Social Security benefits, then you must call the local Social Security office and tell them of his date of death.

This may create a need for you to return some portion of the monthly benefit based on the day of the month he died. If the benefit was set up as an automatic payment to his bank account, then they will submit a reversal to that account to recover that portion of the money that was paid on, perhaps, the third Wednesday of every month in advance of the upcoming month.

At the same time, if you are over the age of sixty, you can apply for a widow's benefit immediately. As mentioned earlier, that money should be automatically deposited into your checking account as soon as possible. What choices you are given and what choices are the most appropriate for your situation are totally dependent on each woman's finances.

If you're still working, you need to let your employer know and work with your advisors to change the beneficiaries on insurance policies, pensions, and other employment benefits. You may reconsider the amounts withheld for retirement plans and adjust deductions for taxes.

NOW WHAT?

So let's assume you got all the benefits you are entitled to, the life insurance has been paid to you, your Social Security has been received, your investment portfolio has been changed to your name, and now you need to know how to spend your money.

Before you know how you will spend it, you must decide on a temporary income need and a permanent income need. Let me define both: a temporary income need is what you will have to have on an annual basis to *remain* in your current living arrangements, and the permanent income need is an ambiguous number based on where you decide to live on a permanent basis.

It is possible to have both at the same time. You need to pay the bills where you are or move immediately to another form of living arrangement, such as a subsidized apartment (the rent payment is assisted by the federal government) or a private pay apartment (where you pay the full rent and most likely the utilities yourself).

We financial planners mostly assume in conversations about widowhood that the widow is well and in good, or pretty good, health. But if your husband, now your deceased husband, was your primary caregiver, the loss of this caregiver status as well as his provider status can prove devastating to the best laid plans. The subsidized housing arrangements or assisted living facilities may be the only option you have if you needed this type of help before he died.

Assuming your husband did provide adequate income and assets for your care, and you are capable of living alone, then running to a temporary facility may not be a good idea.

Just stop and take a deep breath.

If the bills can be paid, you have time on your side to make this important decision about where you will live and in what type of living arrangement.

It is important to discuss your options with your children or other family members. They may offer you something that would be more attractive for a number of perfectly good reasons: greater access to cultural events, more land to garden, more activities geared to those in your own age group, educational opportunities you cannot get where you are now, more time to spend with your children and grandchildren, closer availability to places you would love to travel to, better spiritual connections, better medical attention and resources.

None of these are too insignificant to dismiss lightly. The freedom your singleness offers is a relatively new phenomenon, especially to those who have been married for over twenty-five years. Going it alone is not such a bad thing, but having friends and family can help to make it okay.

If, at some point in your life, you have ever wondered what it would be like to live in one or many different places, this may be your chance to go to "wherever," stay in a hotel or inn for a few days, and get to know from the locals what they like and dislike about the place.

Take public transportation to a few areas of the town and see what people are doing and what impression you have of the place: is it dirty, are the people generally happy, do they speak well of the town, do they have generations of family that stay here, what are their favorite parts of the town, how many people are there your age in the area and what do they do for fun, what is the cost of living in the area, is the health care adequate, poor, or fantastic, what is the temperature range, do they have any new condos and homes or are they old single family dwellings that are in need of repair (not a bad thing if you are into the restoration of old homes). You will have a sense of the place and can rate it on a scale of one to ten.

Then do that again to another couple of places that have caught your eye or piqued your interest. And before you buy anywhere, stay there a couple times in different seasons if you have the time to do that. Please do not buy a place the first time you visit. Too many people have regretted that decision and then found they could not sell the property for what they paid for it. To help you narrow your choices down to someplace more in line with all the questions just put forth, try the quiz for free on www.findyourspot.com, a wonderful source of information that asks for your input on key questions, asks some more, and then suggests several places on this great planet that might appeal to you.

At the same time, consider what you would be leaving behind. I have often encouraged clients to make a T list. On the left side list all the advantages; on the right side, all the disadvantages. Then, one by one, look carefully at each item on your list and rate each of them from one to three with three being the most important or attractive and one being the least important or attractive. Do the same on the right side. Then see which of the issues are most important and least important to you. And then put the paper away. Come back to it in a few months and try it again without looking at the responses you wrote previously. Then compare your responses.

The reason for this second attempt is purely because of the emotional changes you will have experienced in the intervening months. Your pain and fear may have lessened and your priorities will change as you move through the emotions of the loss of your husband. What you thought you needed a few weeks after his death will probably not be the same as what you think you need a few months after his death when hopefully the former dull, fuzzy aimless way of life has yielded to a more logical and stable person.

Or maybe not.

Grieving is a strange cup of tea. It ebbs and flows like a mixed-up stream, and the decisions you think are the right ones one day can be the wrong ones the next. When you can feel it in your gut that this is the right thing to do, move forward. If it seems like the right thing to do for your children's sake and your extended family's sake, it probably isn't the right thing for you.

I am no grief counselor and do not want to assume that I know this state of mind, but having witnessed it in two intimate situations in my mother's life, I know it was chaotic at best, gut-wrenching at worst. And who she was in the first part of the process was not who she was in the later parts of the process; nonetheless, she endured. She has now relocated to another residence in another part of this state and is taking it all with great equanimity and grace. Not so, in the initial phase of this transition in her life. But it feels right for her and so it shall be. By the way, she did the T list, and this move was the result of that exercise.

Back to the financial issues: the temporary budget will allow you to buy time. The permanent budget will give you peace of mind and a place to call home. Both are relevant. If you work with a good planner, he or she can help you to recall all the possible spending items that make up a well-rounded life. Refer to the Living Expenses Worksheet in this book to give you a great resource on what items people spend money on and what percentage of your total spending should be allocated to what types of expenses.

Don't be afraid to admit you made a mistake in your choice of living quarters. Perhaps you really feel that you made too rash a decision and want to return to your former residence. If you sold the house, you are out of luck, but there are others for sale that might bring you to the old neighborhood or at least the town you lived in. Nothing in life is permanent. Except death and taxes …

But please give it time before you make a move. Transitions don't happen automatically or in the course of a few weeks. Get out and get active in your community. Try the restaurants; try the churches, synagogues, temples; try the community colleges and senior centers; try the volunteer organizations. Give yourself an arbitrary time line to experience what you have in front of you.

If you really are unhappy and it has everything to do with the choice of residency you made rather than the state of widowhood, remember you can always go back. If it is about the emotional challenges of widowhood, please get some counseling, because it will go with you no matter where you live.

So let's move forward and see what you will now do with your single life. Will you go back to work, will you volunteer, will you go back to school to get an education, will you do some part-time work to learn a new job or career? Will you be the in-house babysitter?

Widowhood is also a time to set boundaries. If babysitting your grandchildren is a real pleasure to you, then do it. But make sure your children know that you also need to get on with your life as well. Let them know that you are willing to offer them this service, but you want to spend some time with new friends, new church, new career. If you don't, they will unknowingly take advantage of you and assume you will be available at any time. Yes, your grandchildren will grow up and no longer need you. Are you willing to put your life on hold for that? If so, great. If family is the most important part of your life, then being there for your grandchildren should be your priority. If not, then moving in with your children may not be a healthy thing for you to do.

Given that women are living longer, more productive lives, consider the opportunities that await you. My mother-in-law sees widowhood as an opportunity to go out with friends who inspire her with their stories of overcoming their own health issues and those of their children. As widows, they comfort each other and are there for support for each other.

Every Friday, they go to the beauty parlor and get their nails done, their hair washed and set, then a trip to the pizza parlor and food shopping. This routine is helpful in having something to look forward to each week and someone to be accountable to as well. They also go to the movies every Saturday afternoon, then out for dinner someplace in the area, all with the careful driving skills of one of the women who is ninety-two.

They enjoy each other's company and are intellectually stimulated as well. I witnessed that at her ninetieth birthday party when her friends, all of whom are capable of living on their own, without any aids for walking, breathing, or eating, decided that they were there that day to celebrate the birthday of a friend. Talk of their ailments, children's financial issues, or their own problems was off-limits. What a joy it was to be in their company!

The youngest was a girl of eighty-three and the oldest was ninety-five. Life is good. Each one of them had a memorable life with a husband of over fifty years and each misses her man a lot. But they all enjoy the freedom and financial independence they now have to do what they want with their lives and with whom they want to do it. None of them is interested in remarrying and have no need to do that. They are a treat to be around.

If you are experiencing the pain and heartache of widowhood, please know that it is not a sentence of life in prison, continuously mourning the life that could have been, the experiences you will never have the opportunity to know. Widowhood is a temporary state. It is a process that will follow the traditional human emotions of loss: fear, anger, denial, and acceptance. How long you experience each of those phases is directly proportionate to the outlook you have on life.

I hope you will take the time to allow yourself to experience all of it, but be sure to find the joy of life at the end of this difficult road. There are many women who have gone through this and an equal number who not only survived it but chose to create wonderful fulfilled lives after it. Choose the latter for your sake as well as those who love and care about you. And by all means, give yourself permission to enjoy life and do some of the things that you and your late husband would have done with the money you saved had he not passed before you. You'll find plenty of company to share life with.

ACTION STEPS

1. Make a list of the assets you know you have and where they are held.
2. Ask your husband to help you develop that list.
3. Request a meeting with your financial advisor (or get one!) to make sure you understand the plan and the income you might expect if your husband dies first.

NO FEAR ABOUT JOB LOSS

Rarely is anyone prepared for a job loss. The financial part of it is troubling enough; the emotional part is the roughest.

Contrary to the unending psychological review *(what could I have done differently, did it even have anything to do with me, was it something I should have seen coming but didn't want to face)*, the financial aspect of a job loss is as clear as a bell. The abject fear of no income will put most people into a state of mental gridlock. Especially if you are like most Americans and live from paycheck to paycheck. Now what?

Rather than sit around and moan the loss of your job, use it as a time for re-creation, for renewal, for reinvention. This takes some doing psychologically, but for many people this has been the best thing that ever happened to them. Consider a few examples:

A former Wall Street investment banker with a six-figure income and outrageous bonuses gets caught in the web of the sub-prime mortgage mess and is one of many thousands who loses her job. Trying to find another job in the same industry is virtually hopeless since the industry has ceased to exist. And there are thousands like her, unemployed, looking for the same number of jobs in a less than bountiful job pool.

Sally gets a call from a friend who discovers that the former investment banker is no longer taking the 5:30 a.m. train to the city, no longer taking the 7:30 p.m. train home, and has finally taken some time to breathe. Her friend offers her an opportunity to help with a nonprofit that has one paid employee and thousands of requests for help. Given her need to do something from day-to-day, Sally jumps at the chance to be productive.

She finds that not only is she productive but she loves the work she does—the feeling of making a difference and the knowledge that she can't be fired. She is actively raising funds for the organization and keeping her income needs satisfied by doing some consulting for start-up businesses in her area. When asked if she is still looking for a job as an investment banker, her answer is a clear no. She said losing her job was the best thing that ever happened to her and she has never been happier. She does count her pennies and has to look at her finances on a more regular basis than she did before, but she is so much happier and fulfilled that she doesn't care about the six-figure income loss.

Another woman, Patty, who did work in the social service world and was a fund-raiser for two organizations, decided to make a significant change in her life within the same field. In her role as a volunteer for local charities she discovered something that changed her life.

She was struck by the lack of interaction at children's hospitals between those patients who were bed-ridden and those who were mobile and able to access the hospital playroom. She questioned the child life specialists at the hospital as to why certain patients were not brought down to the playroom like the others, and she was told that they could not do that; they were either too ill or too weak or too dependent on the IVs they had attached to their bodies and were unable to be moved.

So she decided to create a portable playhouse and visited on a weekly basis at the bedsides of the children who could not join the others. She contacted a bead manufacturer on Long Island who donated beads of many different colors and textures. She put the beads and the beading supplies in a plumber's toolbox and went from patient to patient to make a beaded necklace or bracelet for the child or for someone else the child chooses.

She has developed this into a national program that selects and trains volunteers to do this at other hospitals who contract with her. The hospitals require all the volunteers to successfully complete their volunteer training program including knowledge of safety issues. She currently has demand from hospitals around the world.

She was so inspired by this work that she discovered in a dream one night the way to raise funds for this venture of love: she would call the *Guinness Book of World Records* and see if anyone had ever done the world's longest beaded necklace. She found they did and wanted to know what the length of the necklace was so she could see if she could beat it. She currently has over 90 percent of the necklace done and will beat the world record by the deadline. But more importantly, she requests that each child "earn" the money to contribute to the necklace and charges $1 per bead. The children love it, the parents love it, and the foundation is getting the funding it needs.

This was truly an inspiration and one that caused her to give up her fund-raising career. She sold a large home, left a good job, and moved to a small rural area to open her charity. She said she has never been happier. Her husband is a laborer who took early retirement and the two of them are content with the life they now lead.

Another woman, Denise, chose to leave a great corporate opportunity to start a small cake decorating business. A former CPA who worked in a large regional firm and was clearly on track for a partnership, she decided that the endless hours of tax season and the frequent trips out of town for corporate clients was way too tiring and not in the least creative. She took her 401k money, her severance package, and her knowledge of business and followed her creative gifts to make cakes for special occasions such as weddings, birthdays, and anniversaries. She is someone who can make her day a non-stop marathon but loves every minute of it. Five years later she is looking for a second store.

The stories go on. But one thing is clear. It takes a great deal of courage to walk away from financial security whether it is by choice or by fate. But more and more American women are beginning to question the value of competing in a corporate world with the same ultimate goals of our male counterparts. How important is that seat on the board of directors, how important is the corner office and a title to go with it, how important is financial success if it deprives you of a balanced life?

And it is not just women who are asking that question. Many men of the next generation are looking at the same issues. More men are giving the responsibilities of fatherhood a greater priority. They are foregoing the move to another city with a promotion in favor of having their wife's career move forward in the same town and placing a greater value on quality time with their spouses and children. We may see this as a good thing for all concerned.

WALK THE EMOTIONAL TIGHTROPE

But what if you find yourself without a job, without a creative urge, and without a burning desire to do good? What do you do with your life?

Let's start with the assumption that you loved the work you did before you were fired, laid off, or jobless for whatever reason. If so, then you might look for the moment at getting another job in the same field as your former job. As my husband did, he took his contact list and reviewed each one to remember under what context he knew the person, made some notes about their families, pets, and so forth and decided, in advance, what he wanted the end result of every conversation to be.

Being a successful sales professional at a high level in the financial information business, he was an expert in attracting and processing business cards he accumulated during his long career. Some were in foreign countries, some in related businesses, some in his own company. But he excluded no one. He often said, "You never know where a contact can take you so don't assume you already know where it will go." It was emotionally difficult to put a smile on his face before every call, but he told me you can "hear" a smile. Good advice.

He prided himself on being a fifty-five-year-old man who successfully landed a great job *in less than three months* after the parent venture capital firm fired the entire senior management of his company. But it was his diligence over the three months after his departure that got him the job. He made it his business to be on the phone from 10 to noon, a break for lunch and for his mental health, then back on the phones at 1:30 to 2:00 and he went to 4:00. He did make it his job to get a job. And it paid off.

Many days it was defeating and frustrating. Many times he wanted to just forget about it and go to the gym. And some days he did just that. Some days he was feeling sorry for himself and just couldn't be the upbeat guy that he knew his contacts expected of him. So he did take a break or two. Don't assume that you must be always up for the task.

Maybe the most important aspect of losing a job is the emotional tightrope. Although it used to be exclusively a male trait, we women now define ourselves with great pride by our job titles, as do the men in our lives. That carries with it a tacit assumption that having achieved a certain level of expertise and acumen, you will always want to enter a new job at the same level or higher than you did in your previous position. And we turn up our noses at jobs that may be of a lower managerial level or in a different field if it does not carry the same cachet as the job title had before. We are, after all, looking to improve our lot in life, not take a step backward!

It's also worth it to ask for your termination benefit package if one is not specifically offered to you. By law, you are entitled to an extension of the health care benefits you had under a program called COBRA. It allows you to pay the premium but keep the same benefit program. So if you were using benefits for a health condition and had already met the deductible, it is a good idea to consider continuing the current plan, unless the new premiums are so high it makes it impossible to carry the coverage.

Under the Affordable Care Act (ACA), it may make sense to buy your own coverage. Please carefully compare the Summary of Benefits and Coverage before you make the switch.

Watch what you do with your 401k plan too. New employers may allow you to roll your existing balance into their own plan, but you will have to get some advice on what plans to enroll in. Unless it was the same company who administered the previous plan, the investment choices will probably be different. JUST MAKE SURE YOU DO NOT TAKE THE CHECK MADE PAYABLE TO YOU, unless you expect to take the money and use it to pay your basic living expenses. They will take a chunk out for income taxes and a 10 percent tax penalty if you are not age fifty-nine and a half when you withdraw the money.

As a better alternative, you can roll the full amount into an IRA Rollover Account at any financial institution you select. That way it is still considered retirement money and not subject to current taxation. And you wouldn't miss a beat. It would be up to you to find someone like me (a Certified Financial Planner) to help you select the proper investment vehicles to manage your retirement plan.

But if we look at possibilities rather than positions, we might find a new breath of life in another company, with more potential for upward mobility. A smaller company might have unique opportunities to expand your skill sets, to gain greater visibility, and break through the proverbial glass ceiling quicker. It may mean a cut in your income, but it may result in increased personal satisfaction and more creative avenues for you to take some risks.

Allowing yourself to experience the attitude of endless possibilities may give you freedom to experiment, to learn some new things about yourself, to move to another part of the country or the world. If you keep yourself on a narrow path to the next higher position within the same industry, you also set yourself up for potential failure if the fundamental business model becomes antiquated or obsolete (newspaper reporting, video rentals, and CD manufacturing are some current deadends).

For many people, we process the loss of a job like most other losses in our lives. Perhaps not fatal losses, but severe emotional losses. Dr. Elisabeth Kubler-Ross in her now-famous litany allows that we all go through stages of loss: denial, anger, bargaining, depression, and acceptance. From the perspective of the book she wrote on this topic, these stages are typical of those who are diagnosed with a terminal illness or upon the death of someone you love, but the phases of loss one goes through can relate to a job loss as well. Perhaps the bargaining part would be somewhat irrelevant, but it could be replaced with questioning your self-worth, then a feeling of being frozen, to finally accepting what is happening.

For those who think that you move right from job to job without experiencing some of the emotional component of loss are fools. We all wonder: *why did it happen to me?* We all need the "exit interview" to get at least the employer's part of the story. But what about the endless wondering what we could have done differently, wondering if the signs were there but we did not see them or chose not to, wondering if the reasons for our firing were inherent personality flaws that we are doomed to repeat, wondering if it was easier just to fire you than to point out the problems you present to employers that you are unaware of, the wondering if you will ever get the truth.

BOUNCING BACK FROM JOB LOSS

Although I am an entrepreneur and have been for most of my life, I did do several stints as an employee. And I was fired twice. The first was for reasons that were obvious to me and from a job I was happy to leave. I had just completed college and signed a lease with my childhood friend and fellow college graduate for an apartment in the area of the college. She was to continue to grad school and I was to be a French teacher. Except the French teacher position was filled in June by a person who had a dual major in French and German. I was previously assured I would have the job of my host teacher since she was retiring that June. And then life got in the way.

The school district felt that they needed someone who had a duel major since language classes were an elective at that time. And not too many people really wanted to learn French, at least not enough to fill the classes. Since the area had a strong population of German immigrants, those German classes would fill up the schedule. So welcome to the real world.

Now I found myself looking for a new job. I answered an ad for a local newspaper circulation department and started working at minimum wage. The old curmudgeon who was in charge of the department issued an order that all women working there (no men applied for that job) would be required to wear skirts or dresses and no "slacks." Right.

I complained that I had just graduated from college and did not have the money to buy new clothes; I felt it was unfair to ask me to go out and buy new clothes on a minimum wage job. He did not agree. And being a freshly-minted feminist, I ungraciously snorted like a pig every time I thought he was out of earshot, but apparently he wasn't. When I was called into his office to be fired, he told me he thought I was rude and disruptive to the other "girls" in the department so I had to go. Obviously, this clothing directive seemed to me like an indignity to all the women in the office. I thought it was totally out of place and occurred to me to be a slap to my own integrity to work for such a beast, so I cheerfully left.

But then the reality of life slammed me in the face. Okay, so now how do I pay my rent and buy food? I took a job at a national low-end department store, which is now defunct. And again, I made minimum wage. I hated it, but I did get along with the manager who was barely a few years older than I. After I had put enough fallen sweaters back on their plastic hangers, I decided to leave the area and move back home.

That's where I had a nervous breakdown and really felt the pain and disappointment of job failure. It hung around me like a cloud. I hated to get up in the morning and I hated to listen to my parents suggesting, then advising, then demanding that I get a job. And as the fates would have it, our life insurance representative stopped by one day with his supervisor to collect the premiums on the little family life insurance policies my parents had. As they are trained to do, the agent and his sales supervisor started asking questions about the family and when the supervisor realized there was an unemployed daughter who had a teaching degree, they said they had a deal for me. Thus began my career in the financial services industry and the rest, as they say, is history.

My second brush with job loss occurred when I was in my early forties, when I left a regional accounting firm. It was more a mutual thing and I actually had a severance package and benefits for a period of time. I had also accumulated some savings and some nice 401k money to take with me. I decided to go back into business for myself at that point, and I went through all my savings, my 401k and my severance. I struggled once again, but I persevered.

The road has been rocky but I thrived in spite of it. I assume that as you mature, you find your own resilience and your belief that it will all work out in the end. It has for me. But at the time of my departure from the accounting firm, I had no idea if I could really pull it off. I went through all the same steps of loss, the fears, the apprehension, the ambiguity, the public face versus the private face.

What if you did not find a job right away—say in six months or less? Now there are additional financial issues to consider. If you did receive a severance package, which would pay you for a period of time based roughly on your length of employment with the company, you should be able to survive for a while without tapping into any personal assets. For some, former employers allow you to collect unemployment insurance as well. That alone will not pay most of the bills, but it helps to fund at least some job search costs.

If you were allowed a period of time with an outplacement service, use that to your advantage. Your daily trips to the outplacement office should be perceived as a full-time job. Go there every day with a plan of action as to what you will accomplish every day. It may not produce a job but it will give you some important résumé-writing advice, interviewing skills, preparedness training, and potential leads. All worth your time and effort.

BUDGET FOR JOB LOSS (BECAUSE YOU NEVER KNOW)

Now more than ever, it is critical that you address your personal finances. Dare I say it, but you need to look at a budget. All right, call it a personal cash flow statement, or whatever it is you need to call it so that you will not be intimidated or scared to death to complete it.

You will need to become familiar with zero-based budgeting, paying out only those expenses you need to survive. The rest of them are to be put in abeyance until some new income sources arrive. These mandatory expenses would include your mortgage or rent, your auto, life, homeowner's (or renter's) and health insurance premiums, any credit card minimum payments, auto lease or loan payments, or home equity loans. Give yourself a budget for food, updated clothing, utilities, auto license, registration, and gasoline. And something for pet food, haircuts, personal care. That's it.

Then look at your severance package, your unemployment insurance payments, and any other sources of income you may have (rental income from rental properties, royalties from patents, consulting income on the side, personal investment income). Now you know how long you can continue to maintain your lifestyle while you look for additional employment. If you've set up a home equity line of credit or you have cash advances available on credit cards, you will have additional sources of income before you have to consider more drastic measures.

Another source of cash might be the cash value of life insurance policies, if you owned that type of policy. Take as much as you can but only up to the point that the life insurance policy can continue to support itself. Your agent can help you with this calculation.

As difficult as it may be to consider this, you must have a plan B. What if the money runs out before you find employment? What are your options? It is much easier to free your mind to find employment when you have a plan B set up in advance. Will it mean you must move in with your children, your siblings, your parents, your best friend? Discuss this possibility in advance so you have some specific offers of assistance before that time arises. But be open to all possibilities. Again, you never know where the help will come from, but putting it out there in the world helps it to find you.

One area of employment that has risen to stardom in the last ten years is outsourcing. It still requires the same skills as an entrepreneur but to a lesser degree. If you haven't done it, you might consider first taking a skills assessment test of any type. Most coaches and outplacement firms will ask you to do this as a basic step.

If you haven't requested your employer to allow you to use the services of an outplacement firm, you might lobby strongly for this. Many times you find that the reason you are no longer employed at the company you left was because your skill sets were not really a match for the job you were asked to do. Kind of like the round peg in a square hole. Your employer may have felt that your experience in your previous position was such that you should have been able to handle the supervisory role you were promoted to. But, in fact, you had no supervisory skills at all or they were your weakest ones. Many employers feel they are doing the right thing by promoting those with experience when, in fact, they are courting disaster, and you take the hit.

As an employer myself, I always have a prospective employee, who may interview well, take a test called Kolbe. It measures skill levels and teaches the employer how to work effectively with an employee to guide and encourage top performance. Without that knowledge I found that I was trying to have an employee complete tasks in the way I would have done so, yet it was totally inappropriate to their personality. With prior registration and user codes, you can take the test yourself online and find out what your skill sets are.

Testing will be helpful for you to isolate what types of jobs you are really good at. It may mean that you need to start looking at different industries, different jobs, or different areas of the country. Say, for instance, you find that you are talented at hospitality, like hotel management, or theme parks. Since they tend to be more in larger cities and many are in the southeast or southwest, you may have to consider relocating.

Or you could find that you are a whiz at crunching numbers and talking to clients, but you have little interest or skills in the marketing area. So you avoid sales and look for a position as a client services representative.

These tests and many like them will guide you to finding not only an area where you can excel but then you can look at salary.com and find out what people are paid for that job in certain areas of the country. There is so much information for free on the web (not just at the traditional job sites but even craigslist.com has free listings).

Needless to say, if you are not computer savvy, now would be the time to get some basic computer skills. Most community colleges offer programs for the novice and for those who feel left behind by technology. Many government-funded programs also offer computer education for those who qualify for the program, such as the Small Business Development Councils at major colleges and universities.

It is amazing what you will find if you really start to look and to ask questions. The sources of free and minimal-cost programs are astounding. Look also at the state-funded programs that offer employment assistance but also provide counseling services and resources you can use.

REINVENTING YOU

Is it time for a total revamp of your career/job history? For many women in their fifties and beyond, it is time to look inside and see if the career path they have embarked on for at least twenty-five years is still making them feel as if they want to get up in the morning and go to work.

For some, the answer is yes and they will be suited up until someone pushes them out. For others, it is the turning point in their lives, when the loss of a job signals the beginning of a new world that is intimately satisfying. They finally feel as if they are making a difference in the world one person at a time, or one organization at a time. The power of reinvention is quickly supplanting the tired search for a new job in the same field they left.

In addition to the women whose stories I wrote about at the beginning of this chapter, there are scores of us who are questioning this rat race we call corporate America. Given the lack of ethical conduct, the greed that allows for a select few to benefit on the backs of ignorant people, the tolerance of the lack of accountability for their actions, the women of America are asking themselves if this is a world they want to play in.

Our hard wiring calls for us to nurture, to find joy in the accomplishment of others, to grow—not destroy—things, to want equal treatment for all, to build things that last for generations, and none of that seems to be the culture-of-the-day in corporate America.

We have lost trust in these venerated institutions and have seen some of the biggest fall. This is not who we are. It is sad to watch the women in high corporate positions mouthing the same inane, scripted responses to the malfeasance and irresponsibility of large institutions. Sad, because it is so not like us to not tell the truth. Women have always been the gatekeepers of our society's morality. And we are losing the right to claim that when we sell our birthright for a seat on the board of directors.

So let's reevaluate what it is we do in this world. As we take more and more of the responsibility for governing these behemoths of industry, we must start looking at what we give up to play the game by the given rules. For those who decide to stay in corporate America, we can insist on adding the values we hold dear to the ethics of doing business.

For those women who are in positions to lead and manage the assets of a corporation, including its employees, we need to add a more humane way to address the natural and evolutionary layoffs of employees. We need to care about what happens to them and to their families because we choose to let them go. Companies need to make sure downsized employees are re-trained for additional employment opportunities, and when a challenger takes out an existing company, the mandate to re-train and include as many employees as possible needs to be the written rule, not the exception.

Yes, it is true that the corporate structure is changing and changing rapidly. Instead of assuming that downsizing is the only option, there is the aforementioned outsourcing. Many senior-level executives are beginning to look at outsourcing as a way to allow former employees to continue to work for the same corporation minus the overhead of keeping them on: the office space, the utilities costs, the unpredictability of commuting to and from the office, the support staff, the top-heavy benefit programs, the unemployment issues, and more.

The outsourced employee is a self-employed contractor who is now responsible for her own office space, utilities, no commuting, support staff (maybe), and all her benefits. Without those costs, outsourcing is the promise of a continuing stream of income since the savings can be passed on in part to the outsourced person. Rather than fire someone who has valuable skills and knowledge of the company, the outsourced person now has the "freedom" to work from home, lower commuting costs, if any, and the ability to be outsourced to more than one company. If it appears that the engagement will not be permanent, then the person has the freedom to engage other similar companies, even their competitors, to perform the same services.

A caution: if you sign a noncompetitive agreement with one employer, you may risk being unable to work with others in the same field (sometimes for up to two years after a layoff or termination or end of a project). Go into these agreements with your eyes wide open. Read anything you sign as a condition of employment.

In doing the research for this book, I came across a website with an article that lists the "Top 25 Places to Find a Freelancer," and it is a valuable resource for those who want to be listed. Freelancing gives you the ability to earn an income for your knowledge and design a life that has some balance. This area of business is the fastest growing piece. More and more employers are becoming highly interested in "virtual employees" rather than in the layers and layers of "permanent" employees with all their performance issues, discrimination issues, and all the other human resources problems that masses of people present.

IN WITH OUTSOURCING

The visionaries of American business are moving to a model of a three-tier business:

1.   A small group of high-level executives responsible for core departments,
2.   A level of outsourced employees who can provide the enhanced but vital components of doing business (IT, HR, PR, advertising, and so on), and
3.   The temporary workers who are there for a given period of time to provide a service.

Since our country has moved most of the manufacturing business offshore, our future growth will come in the services realm: financial, computer technology and support, health care, elder care, business consulting, among others. Again, if you have the skill sets of a business service (such as accounting, customer service, marketing, graphic design, IT, personnel training), these skills can be contracted out on an outsourcing basis. And the freelancers who can work on a project basis can be free to move around as situations and factors in our economy change.

The largest outsourcing occurs now in Asia and India with thousands of newly trained English-speaking (barely) phone jockeys handling most of the IT support and customer service departments for major U.S. corporations. They work for less than our minimum wage and can balance the differences in the foreign time zones of Americans to be available 24/7. Our economy is truly global. What was once the exclusive domain of the lowest paid Americans has now been replaced by a full population who will take less than our minimum wage to sustain a better-than-average standard of living in other parts of the world.

This trend will continue. If this is where you were formerly employed, it is time to consider a whole new career track because these services will not be coming back to our shores anytime soon.

But change here is a good thing. It is this type of harsh business reality that outsourcing forces us to look at. We need to reevaluate our options, and in most cases, it produces a new area of business for those whose jobs were sent abroad.

HOME-BASED SWEET HOME

Another out-of-the-box approach to jobs is the home-based business. The growth in home-based businesses has been astounding in this country. The websites are too numerous to mention, but the opportunities are boundless. As our country continues to employ both husbands and wives, or if your job is so all-encompassing that you don't have the time to be a wife and an executive (like me!), our greater need is for time.

Time is the commodity we have the least of. That's why now is the time to enter service businesses. They are all worth mentioning if only for one reason: they require minimal amounts of capital (money) to get into them, and the freedom to expand the business, or not, is totally up to you.

If you are frustrated about not finding the right job and would consider the idea of starting your own business, here are only a few to get your brain really moving:

- Home inspection
- Residential and commercial cleaning (you don't have to do it, just supervise!)
- Dry cleaning
- Car detailing
- Résumé writing
- Business broker
- Interpreter
- Virtual office assistant (I use one for bookkeeping and one for transcribing)
- Personal chef
- Caregiver relief
- Publicist
- Copywriter
- Wedding or event planner
- Dog walker/groomer
- Personal shopper
- Food delivery
- Home inventory business (you record information that could be vital if a natural disaster strikes)
- Interior decorator
- Silk flower designer
- Candy portrait designer
- Or any number of franchises that don't cost an arm and a leg

It is amazing to me, as a member of the National Association of Women Business Owners (NAWBO), how many women have created businesses based solely on the skills they know they have and the pure joy of doing what they do. Maybe they don't make a fortune, but they learn from each other how to do things more effectively and they use the talents and skill sets of other members to help them succeed.

Yes, some have failed. But more of them succeed because of the collaborative nature of women. We help each other get better and act as a free resource to each other. We mentor. We support. We celebrate each other's minor and major accomplishments. And the types of businesses, most of which are started at home, flourish and become the employers and business leaders of tomorrow. Their stories are all unique, but their desire to succeed, raise a family, and, for many, have a great marriage, are inspirational.

If you are thinking of starting a business, consider first the free services of the Small Business Development Councils in your area, usually associated with larger universities and colleges, and then join NAWBO (www.nawbo.org). Your chances of succeeding increase dramatically with both those resources behind you.

As I wrote earlier, the stories of women who left corporate America and decided to go it alone are impressive, but be reasonable. If you are not someone who is self-directed and who needs the structure of an office environment, owning a business is probably not your best alternative to searching for another job. But there's nothing to say you can't try something from your home while you are looking. How hard can it be to be a personal shopper or a food delivery person for someone who does not have the time to do either? If you charge the right amount of money, it is something to help you financially as well. Find some task you enjoy doing and offer it to others. Who knows, you may love it so much you decide to hire others and a business is born!

One of the most memorable transformations I experienced personally was that of a woman, Nancy, who had been a full-time mother of three, one of whom was deaf. Rather than allow her deaf daughter to be isolated and surrounded by other deaf children, she and her husband decided to mainstream their daughter while her mother sat with her in every class and "signed" what the teacher was saying. That allowed her daughter to participate in life and to have the self-confidence to see herself not as a handicapped person, but as a person who had a physical challenge.

Her daughter went on to graduate from college (without her mother present in every class!) and to get a full-time job in a large metropolitan city and live on her own. She is fully integrated into so-called normal society and continues to prosper.

Several years later, Nancy suffered a heart attack at age forty-four while on a vacation in the islands and survived, determined to translate her healthy cooking skills, learned from her grandmother, into a business as a personal chef. She shadowed chefs from New York and New Jersey and then decided to start her own business. She has taken the business all the way from a "good idea" to that of a wildly successful venture. She goes to clients' homes with a menu and a grocery bag full of food and prepares meals for a week. She has had to turn away business because she can't handle any more new clients.

That inability to handle the demand did spur her on recently to buy a commercial kitchen so that she could make the meals en masse and then deliver them to clients, which will allow her business to expand. Her business combined two deep passions: the love of good food and the desire to make families healthy. She had no formal business experience or culinary training. With the support of other NAWBO members, she found the knowledge and skills needed to develop a business, get the funding, find the clients, discover the marketing experts, and she was on her way.

Another area to explore when job searching is to partner with someone who has a different set of skills but in the same industry. For example, a woman who is great at web design can partner with someone who is adept at social networking (Twitter, Facebook, LinkedIn and whatever is next). Or a bookkeeper can partner in a virtual assistant package with someone who is good at doing tax returns. A transcriptionist can partner with someone who is a skilled interpreter. You get the idea. Your double set of skills, not to mention your double sets of contacts, could easily make the search for outsourcing opportunities that much more effective.

And the beauty of the Internet makes finding those partners all the easier, especially if you both formerly worked for the same large company and now find yourselves in different parts of the country. If you have some skills you are thinking of outsourcing, register on the website of the International Virtual Assistants Association (www.ivaa.org). This will give you tons of info on how to register, how to price your services, how to advertise for specific geographic areas, how to market your services, and more. It's a wonderful resource for those who are ready to slow down and want the world to know what you do and how many hours a week you want to work.

TURN JOB LOSS INTO A JOB GAIN

If nothing else, please remember that losing a job is not always a bad thing. It may look like it at the time, but you have been given an opportunity to look deep within yourself and reinvent yourself if you want to.

Our current society's values are moving away from the promise of a thirty-five-year career with a pension at the other end of the road to a life lived in stages. Some of it may be the first twenty years where we develop some important business skills, and then the next twenty where we move on to test the waters, and the next twenty to arrive at something that we love to do, that makes us want to get up out of bed every day and go to whatever it is that will consume our day with great enthusiasm and joy. Although not every day will be like that, hopefully, there will be many more than before.

Lest that moment of panic happens to you in the near future, start now to accumulate money in a savings account or money market fund that will allow you to sustain your current standard of living for about six months. You know what your bills are each month and then add 20 percent to that total. This is the money you need to have to stave off the wolves while you decide what path your life will take. Please consider the possibility of a new life in a new career or activity as well as just replacing the job you lost. Make some lemonade out of lemons.

ACTION STEPS

1. Review your résumé for updated skills and responsibilities.
2. Have a professional review your résumé for strong verbs to describe your recent accomplishments and team accountabilities.
3. Determine how much you might need to make it through six months if you did lose your job and start a separate fund to accumulate that amount.
4. Consider what tasks you could do and charge for that service to supplement income or start a side business now.
5. Locate an outplacement firm in your area and have an interview with a counselor to learn more about their services and see if they can begin to test you now for your skill sets.
6. Think about ways you might start a home-based service business or outsource your skills.

NO FEAR ABOUT DIVORCE

We are kickin' them out and kickin' butt! The divorce rate among Boomer women is at an all-time high. And it's the women who are pulling the plug.

One of two marriages will end in divorce. A sobering fact. The most common reason is sexual incompatibility or infidelity, whichever comes first. More often than before, the reason is a surprising twist: homosexuality.

Susannah is a woman in her early sixties whose husband, Adam, confessed to her last month that he had deceived her for all these years. She discovered he had a gay lover living in another city a few hours away from them. She never suspected anything because she thought they had had a great marriage, blessed by two sons, two daughters-in-law, and four grandchildren, all who lived within a day's journey from them.

Adam told her he feared alienation from her and their children if he confessed his alternate life and kept it a secret until recently. She wondered what had changed that forced him to feel the need to "ruin her life" with this revelation.

He told her his lover had developed AIDS and he was afraid he might be carrying the HIV virus too. Since she and her husband had not had intimate relations in years, she never thought it was anything out of the ordinary. She believed it was due to a natural loss of sex drive in older people. She did not care about it, and their separate bedrooms proved a wonderful solution for her insomnia and his snoring.

Why should she suspect anything was amiss? His part-time sales job took him to many places in their area, and whatever visits Adam and his lover had must have been during the day because he was home every night.

She called me because she was concerned about the financial losses she would face if they divorced, and she was not ready to agree to that. What, she wondered, did couples do who still cared for each other but chose to live separately? Or together? Adam was still confused about what steps he needed to take because he was not interested in divorce either. He was aware of the fact that many couples remain together and live separate lives with or without legal paperwork.

She did not know if he would continue his lifestyle freely and out in the open. If so, she could not live with that and told him so. He realized his lover would soon die and the whole thing might end there. What to do?

I recognized the delicacy of this situation and, not wanting to practice psychology without a license, I asked her to come in and talk with me. I asked her to consider her life without Adam from a financial perspective. She said if they stayed married, he had a pension, which they expected to receive in a few years that would allow for a survivor's benefit if he predeceased her. Which she acknowledged might happen if he had contracted AIDS. She said he had not yet been tested but promised her he would do so the following week. I suggested she do the same. At first she was horrified at the suggestion, but soon saw the logic in that.

Second, she said she had her own 401k, as did Adam. They both named each other as the beneficiary of their own plans. I showed her how to calculate the monthly benefit she could expect to receive from hers and his. She reasoned all that was sufficient with Social Security to sustain them both if they lived together. Living apart, it would pose a problem.

I suggested she consider the really important question: Could she live under the same roof with him? And if not, then we need to consider some alternatives, including divorce. I strongly suggested they meet with a family counselor and try to work out their feelings and future together before she made any decisions in regard to their retirement assets.

She thanked me for the advice and promised to call me in the near future. The end result to all this was a decision to stay together as a married couple but to continue to live separate lives. He said he could not deny his feelings for other men but promised he would not date or meet other men anywhere in their area.

Susannah was emotionally devastated and could not even consider dating any other man. Fortunately, they both tested negative for HIV/AIDS.

She decided she enjoyed her life as it was and looked forward to spending her retirement with her children and grandchildren and pursuing some other hobbies and interests she had put aside while focusing on her career.

MOVING ON BUT WHY?

While this is not typical of most couples, it is a reminder that we need to consider many reasons for staying in a marriage, not the least of which is financial. Regardless of the reason for the divorce, the couple realized it was more costly to divorce and split their assets than to remain in a reasonable but imperfect relationship for their own sakes rather than the typical reason, for the sake of the children.

Should we start laying blame? How could this be? The ones who were the keepers of the hearth, the earth mother, the embracing woman at the front door (wrapped in cellophane?) would consider leaving the nest?

And of course, there are those who would blame the feminist movement for this mutiny. It might have something to do with giving women the courage and social permission to make the move. Maybe it has something to do with the fact that we are living longer and the thought of spending the rest of our lives in a loveless marriage is unacceptable.

External factors are at play here too. A study commissioned by *AARP The Magazine* showed some phoenix-like reasons for the splits. The commission cited women, who after thirty years or more of living with their husbands, decided that the time was right to move on and live the rest of their lives either unencumbered by a spouse or find the man (or woman) of their dreams. Divorce and remarriage have less social stigma attached to them than they did in the past.

Unfortunately, there is still the uncomfortable statistic of the survival of second marriages being less than 30 percent, but there are also different reasons for marriage in late mid-life, as opposed to those second marriages that happen in your twenties and thirties. Older women and men tend to be more emotionally secure and less inclined to marry for the sake of being married. It is more a choice, than a need.

Women with careers often find themselves in situations where other attractive men or women interact with them socially and intellectually. The image of the housewife happily tending to her home and children and dependent on her husband for financial security and social contacts is more the exception than the rule.

At the same time, women are creating separate lives and circles of friends that do not include their husbands. The need for financial security from a husband is not only diminishing but vanishing. As more women earn a living that equals or exceeds that of their husbands, the power in the relationship is shifting. He (now, she) who holds the power of the purse, rules!

It's a fascinating role change. How does a woman who is the primary breadwinner retain her feminine, passive side in the personal relationship but still take pride and responsibility for her money-making expertise in the financial aspect of the relationship? As usual, we Boomers are setting new standards and, too often, the fall-out is divorce.

Many psychologists feel that this role reversal is contrary to the way we are hard-wired and is destined to create disharmony and separation. Was it not the role of the man to go out into the highlands and kill the beast that provided the food and sustenance for his mate and family? Isn't that still the natural order of things in the animal kingdom?

But there are species of mammals where the female does the killing for the food and brings it back to the lair. She waits until the father of her offspring and her children are fed and she takes the leftovers. He provides the physical security from outside marauders and other external threats, but she is the one who provides the food and raising the young. Sound familiar?

Many women are earning less than or the same as that of their current husbands. Yet women who are in a physically or emotionally abusive, or empty marriage, often choose sanity and peace of mind over the financial security they once had. Women are far more adaptive to life changes than men. We find a way to make it work and soon learn that our singleness can often be a life-saver, literally.

Some interesting statistics on this new phenomenon: according to the AARP study, the women who "walked" were more likely to "emerge[d] from the ordeal of later-life divorce far happier and emotionally healthier than most would have dared to hope at the outset."

And, the survey noted, the number one fear that keeps most people in a bad marriage is the fear of loneliness. Yet a full 75 percent of the women in the survey reported having a serious relationship within two years after the divorce—some even before the divorce was final. Could that be because we are more likely to be emotionally supported by our women friends than men are with their golfing buddies?

A client shared with me recently that her greatest fear of leaving her husband was the potential financial, practical, and social losses. Once she realized that she would be okay financially, have a roof over her head, and some money to live a life without worry, she blossomed. She began writing music, a gift she had ignored in favor of being the corporate wife. She has received scholarships and grants to pursue her dream along with opportunities in New York to write for plays and light musicals.

The one funny thing she shared with me was the inevitable car issues. Since her husband had always taken care of their cars, she never realized that she had to have a car inspected until a trooper pulled her over and told her the inspection sticker had expired. She was confused and flustered until he showed her the sticker on the windshield and the need to get it replaced. She realized that these were the "little things" she could certainly do by herself and survive.

The first time she bought a car was a scary experience as well, until we helped her discover what type of car she needed and how to pay for it. It's these little things that can derail even the most "put together" woman. But thankfully there are those who can help.

HOW TO MOVE ON

How do we prepare ourselves for this possible transition at a precarious time in our lives? First and foremost, we make some extremely simple, but subtle, changes to our lives now. If you are in a more traditional marriage where your husband makes all the financial decisions, resolve to be more informed.

The first thing you can do is to review, or in some cases, create a credit history. All of us are entitled to one credit report at no cost each year. It is easy then to see what others see when considering offering credit to you. You can go to www.annualcreditreport.com, among other sites, and order one.

Be sure to review all the entries first to see if there are any fraudulent accounts and second to see if the information regarding your accounts is correct. You can see all the recent credit history, including a report on how often you have made late payments, when an account is in dispute, and how many accounts you have that are open but never used, closed by you, or closed by the issuer. It can be daunting to see all of it and understand their shorthand with symbols, letters, and footnotes, but forge ahead. It is a volume of information that will make a huge difference to you in the future. Your credit report goes with you for a long time.

And what if you don't have any credit cards? If you share all your credit cards in both names, get one in your name only. Heresy, you say? This will cause an immediate divorce, you fear! Not necessarily. You can go to any department store, credit card company, or gasoline company and apply for the card in your own name. If you have a paid position anywhere, you can do this by yourself.

Once you get the card, use it. If you are not a wage earner, you can apply for and get a credit card in your name by using your husband's earnings and employer for reference. He may find out about it, but you might tell him that you are concerned about having no credit in your own name.

The reason for doing this is simple yet powerful. If your husband divorces you (or you divorce your husband), you will not be able to use your existing credit cards if the cards were based solely on his earning capacity. Most of us use department store credit cards to begin with but know that the interest rates on those cards are among the highest in the business. Try to get a bank card (one issued by, for example, Bank of America or American Express), even if it has a low spending limit.

Put some expenses on the card and pay it off the next month. Ah, there's the rub! You must pay it off every month. If you use the cards and pay them off each month, you are creating a credit history in your own name, which can prove to be invaluable later. As you create a solid history of using these cards, call the issuer every couple months and ask for an increase in your spending limits. The more credit you have, the easier the transition out of the house will be. And please, ladies, do not have the card issued in the name of Mrs. John Smith. Make sure you are Mary Smith. Period.

If all your checking and savings accounts and investment accounts are in joint name, start one for yourself. All of this will have to be disclosed on a standardized form should a divorce become a reality, but there is no reason to have everything in joint names. If you need cash while a divorce is in progress, having access to an account in your own name saves you the trouble of asking your lawyer to contact his lawyer to approve the withdrawal or use of the funds. One lawyer recommends that you create a new checking account in your own name at a bank where your husband does not bank.

In addition to your own checking account, get a post office box and your own free email account (Yahoo! and Google will both give you free Internet addresses). Here's why.

Once you establish a checking account in your own name, use it and have your bank or investment statements sent to you online or to the new post office box. Once you drop the bombshell of the impending divorce, you need to work with an attorney who will advise you of how to take half of these accounts in your own name.

If you suspect that your spouse will try to clean out all your checking and savings and investment accounts, you should consider taking half of the assets you have in joint checking or savings accounts and put them in your new account. You can use them to pay for your personal living expenses and show a history of paying your utility, car, and other expenses from it.

You must let your attorney know of your actions and make sure you keep track of the bills you pay from this account. You cannot hide this from the reconciliation of your assets and expenses once you go to settlement, but at least you can avoid having a spouse clean out your checking and savings accounts and leaving you with no money to pay bills. Remember, half of the money, not all of it!

Another recommendation is to get your own cell phone. Getting a cell phone in your own name is extremely easy to do. I can attest to that. Several years ago, some unscrupulous individuals used my Social Security number (I have no idea how they got it) to get not one but three cell phones, ran up the charges and promptly moved on to the next unsuspecting person. I was left with three items on my credit report deemed "uncollectible" and a significant ding on my credit score.

If they can get a phone that easily, so can you. (Please use your own Social Security number, thank you!) And once again, have the bills sent to your email account or your post office box. DO NOT get a phone by adding a line to your husband's account. Kinda defeats the purpose, no?

Of course, all of this presumes that you and your husband are reasonable nonviolent adults—anger and finger-pointing aside. In the case of physical abuse, please contact a domestic violence shelter advocate or counselor before you do any of these tasks. Should your spouse find out that money moves have been made, it could further exacerbate the anger and result in consequences none of us would wish on anyone. Please be careful in how you protect yourself financially but protect yourself physically first.

If you are unemployed, consider a job search now. Look at the volumes of information on the web. Consider taking some preliminary assessments to determine your areas of interest and how they could translate into a paying job. There are a slew of "life coaches," some legit and some frauds, who can help you see what your areas of probable success might be. They can interpret these assessments and help you find some areas where your talents and strengths might be put to use. There is no guarantee that you will start out making tons of money, but you may decide you have indeed found something that you love to do and, incidentally, pays well.

If you don't have a computer at home or fear that your husband may try to see what sites you've visited ("browsing history"), go to your local library. Most libraries have access to the Internet so you can go there to avoid having your browsing history reviewed by your husband. Ask at the library help desk how to "clear your browsing activity." If you are a college alum, consider calling your alma mater to see if their career counselors can give you some free advice.

Maybe simply getting an upgrade to your previous career track is in order. If you had a teaching degree, find out from your state if your certificate is still valid. If not, find out what you need to do to get it there. If your career was nursing, find out again what you need to do for a refresher course or consider using that experience as a way to enter a new career. Maybe you were a hospital nurse who would like to be a school nurse or become a nurse practitioner. If that's the case, there are many opportunities to get college scholarships for women who have been out of the work force for a minimum of ten years.

If you need to go back to school to upgrade your career, check into scholarships that were never available when you went to school the first time around. There are those who make a business in finding some of the most arcane of scholarships and grants to give to those who qualify. Don't give up if you exhaust the more traditional loans and grant opportunities.

Can you turn your hobbies into something that makes money? Are you a great cook? Can you see yourself being a personal chef—someone who cooks meals in advance for others and either delivers them to the client's home or sells them behind a counter? There are franchises for this as well. I am not recommending this to further the role of women in the kitchen but for those who have a real love of cooking, this could be a way to make some money while helping others.

Look into the many franchises with a bent to the unique skill sets developed by women. If you have spent your entire career in a corporate climb, maybe the idea of striking out on your own would be appealing. I know women who are making a killing on Etsy (handmade crafts) or selling on eBay.

We all know stories of women who have dropped out of a competitive world and chosen a softer, more personally satisfying livelihood. Before you drop everything and think of yourself as an entrepreneur, consider a wonderful website devoted to helping you vet your idea and work with a business development coach over the phone known as Biz Starters (www.Bizstarters.com).

In addition to that resource, the federal government has a program for retired senior corporate people and retired small business owners called SCORE, the Service Corps of Retired Executives. This is a free resource and one that has won acclaim over its many years of service to American business owners. They can help you with the finer points of running a profitable business while you concentrate on the product or service you sell.

THE PROCESS ITSELF
(GOOD, BAD, AND UGLY)

How about the mechanics of divorce? How can you be prepared before you go to the lawyer's office? Is there a way to minimize the cost of divorce and save both you and your husband some serious moolah in the process?

Many articles exist on the web to help prospective divorcees be prepared for the split. First you must do some detective work. Gather all your information and important documents. It is best to have these copied and either saved somewhere other than in your home or copied to a CD to keep elsewhere. Either way, you need to have your will, your mortgage and home equity loan paperwork (or if paid off, a copy of your deeds of ownership), your income taxes, your auto loans and/or deeds, statements of checking, savings, and investment accounts, birth certificates, Social Security cards, passports, and any other important records that show your identity and ownership of assets.

If you and your spouse are still on speaking terms, it is to your advantage to try to work out a settlement on your own. One of the biggest hurdles in doing the split is determining the ownership of each of your assets, and which ones would be included in a divorce. In general, assets held jointly are included in your marital assets. Pension plans that were active while married—both yours and your husband's—IRAs, 401ks, and former employer plans sitting there doing nothing are all fair game. If you don't know what your husband has, then it might be more difficult to work on a settlement yourself.

A process called discovery—a legal request for an itemization of all assets held in joint and sole name—would resolve this. It is difficult for each person's attorney to get the truth from each party if one or both of them is withholding information. This failure to disclose is considered a crime. The process of discovery is one of the biggest money drains in a divorce proceeding as each side attempts to verify and account for the assets held by each party.

If you can do this assessment yourself, there is more money left for you both to share. Don't let anger and resentment get in the way of resolving this delicate issue, because both of you will be much the poorer if you leave it to your attorneys to battle it out forever.

On the other hand, giving in for the sake of getting this behind you is not advantageous either. When I met with a divorce attorney recently to gather updated information for this book, she confirmed what I had suspected about the behavior of women in divorce: they either want to punish their husbands (for whatever transgressions he made) or to give up everything to get it over with and move on. Both have significant drawbacks and lead to a lot of regret, as well as a lot of money left on the table.

There is no denying that divorce is an intensely emotional event. But to the degree that you can see it as a business transaction and not a forum for your grievances, the probability of having a settlement you can both live with increases.

In selecting an attorney to represent you, make sure the one you pick has the experience in family law to know when to punt and when to dig in. This is invaluable since once the ink is dry on the settlement, you must live with the terms for the rest of your life. Many husbands' attorneys count on the noncombative nature of women to eventually surrender to the terms offered by their husbands. An aggressive attorney in your corner will help to make sure you get what you deserve, rather than allow you or your children to be forced to compromise.

Experience in divorce laws is important, but so is the ability to represent you in litigation in front of a jury. Some divorce attorneys have strengths in the former but not in the latter. If you expect this to be a contentious matter, choose an attorney with a good reputation in the courtroom.

Then the more difficult part of this process is determining what income is to be considered in the divorce. I know of a client whose husband is a self-employed professional. He intentionally created the impression of a business loss to guarantee that his soon-to-be ex-wife's counsel could not use more than his current income to base his alimony payments to her. This will probably not work in the long run since she was responsible for providing the collateral he needed for the financing to start his business.

She also worked for free in the business in an administrative capacity but is now without a job and an income. She told me she felt like she was fired by her husband in two realms, as a wife and as an employee.

Beware if your husband is a business owner. Being self-employed allows for many secret paths to move otherwise taxable income away from the bottom line. A local attorney reminded me to consider three other sources of assets and future income, which most wives of self-employed business owners forget:

1.   Stock option plans (the ability of your husband to buy stock in the company he works for or owns), which may or may not be exercised,

2.   Deferred compensation plans (programs to intentionally not take income in the current year in which it was earned and defer it until retirement), which will not show up on the books of the company because they are considered "unfunded liabilities," and

3.   The defined benefit pension plan, a type of retirement plan that has no assets to show but will pay monthly a fixed dollar amount to the employee once he or she retires and pay that income for life.

Don't forget "offshore" investment accounts that were created in the Cayman Islands, the Bahamas, the island of Nevis, Switzerland, and others. These accounts are designed to escape the eyes of the IRS, and although they may be legitimately created, they should be considered as part of the assets you acquired during the marriage. But good luck trying to discover them! They intentionally don't show up on tax returns, and the statements are often sent to locations where you wouldn't see them, such as to a summer home, to a mailbox out of town, or to a relative sworn to secrecy.

Having copies of your previous tax returns is more than important; it is vital. If you don't have them, contact the IRS and get copies. There is a wealth of information regarding income on these returns, which could show investment income from accounts you didn't know existed. Unfortunately, too many women just sign the tax returns each year and have no knowledge of what they signed.

Since most women are the payers of the household bills, can you figure out what it would cost you to live after a divorce? This is critical information for you to take to your attorney or to discuss with your husband.

Contrary to what most people think, a divorce does not create a simple 50 percent reduction in expenses. It is more like only a 30 to 40 percent reduction. A good percentage of living expenses are fixed. And they count for about 40 to 50 percent of the total predivorce living expenses.

Think about it: a mortgage is about 30 to 35 percent of your total expenses (and these days it is becoming greater!), your real estate taxes another 5 percent, your car loan about 3 percent, and insurance (auto, life, health) about 10 percent. That doesn't leave much for food, clothing, transportation, utilities, and personal care. So don't expect that living on your own will be half of what it now costs.

There's the real core of the issue. Most people find that living with a spouse is like living with a roommate: two people sharing the fixed costs leaves more for personal spending. By doubling the fixed expenses in two separate residences, you really need to consider if you can afford to maintain your current lifestyles.

There simply is not enough money to create two separate and equal lives. Both suffer financially in a divorce. For a husband to make alimony and child support payments plus create a separate home means significantly less in the net paycheck for him. For the wife, it is rarely enough to maintain the minimums for the children let alone her needs.

But when the divorce occurs in later life, after the kids are gone, and when the wife can devote her time to her own pursuits, the separate living costs are far less. This is why so many women are looking at (or waiting for?) divorce in middle age.

You will need to create a budget (there's that ugly word!) to see what income you will need to sustain a comfortable lifestyle. If you live in a state that does not allow for alimony, you will need to really look at how you can create this separate life. New jobs, career moves, part-time jobs will greatly enhance your financial security. By creating the budget, you will see where you need to supplement your income, if at all.

Consider the types of expenses most of us have. I have often counseled my clients to put their expenses in one of three categories, which I've mentioned in chapter 5, but let's list them again:

- Fixed, for those that will occur regularly in both frequency and amount (rent or a mortgage, or insurance premiums)

- Variable, for those expenses that are necessary but will fluctuate with use (food, clothing, utilities)

- Discretionary, those that represent your specific lifestyle (vacations, pet care, household refurnishing, haircuts)

Once you have outlined all these expenditures of cash, then look to see what percentage each category holds to the total. To be living within your means, or at least comfortably, you should have no more than 35 percent of all expenses within fixed, up to 35 percent in variable, and the remaining 30+ percent for your discretionary expenses.

If you don't fit that profile now, take a closer look at the nature of the distorted percentages; for instance, college education costs, which will end in a few years, unusual medical bills that will cease sometime soon, or too many weddings and graduation gifts in this last year.

Be sure to bring your Living Expenses Worksheet with you when you meet with your attorney. This will help determine what income you will need after your divorce. (The worksheet is located in chapter 5.)

This exercise is often used in bargaining to determine which expenses each spouse will be responsible for in the future. Get a head start on yours by figuring this out yourself.

A MODERN DAY SCARLET LETTER

How about the emotional aspects of divorce? Many Boomers were raised in a family where the idea of a divorce was unacceptable, even sacrilegious. The old adage "you made your bed now lie in it" still haunts many women. Divorce was considered an unacceptable situation for our parents.

Thankfully our society views divorce somewhat differently now. Those we considered to be the stalwarts of the faith showed us that divorce, although not condoned, is now an acceptable option. Divorce was simply not a possibility in previous generations. It was as reviled as the scarlet letter in Hester Prynne's time.

The sense of failure is still present in the psyches of those who do divorce. As long as we continue to define ourselves as single, married, widowed, or divorced, the stigma will endure. Why is it necessary to institutionalize our past relationships when those who remain single and have serial relationships are not required to acknowledge them? We also find some amusement in noting those who have had more than two marriages. Does it make a difference?

In all these scenarios, we are now currently single and the anthology of our past should not be a determining factor in our interactions with the world. Is being a widow nobler than being a woman who cared for an alcoholic for years or a woman who suffered abuse in a marriage for the sake of the children? I suspect in time this distinction will go away as our society cares less for the formality of marriage and more for the well-being of its members. As it is now, the birth rate to unmarried couples matches that of those who got hitched first. I am not advocating the demise of marriage but merely observing the trend. Whether this is a good thing or a bad thing, only time will tell.

Remember when the woman all America loved and revered was filing for divorce from the wealthiest man in the world, Aristotle Onassis? The woman who Catholic America held as the icon of the sacrament of marriage was facing excommunication from the very institution she revered. Yet Jackie Kennedy Onassis wanted out. What would the Vatican do? They brought out a dusty old convention called annulment. That would allow her to say the marriage never really happened and all was right with the Holy Father. Really?

It made no difference what the reason was or how the church reacted. The precedent was set. Catholics living in bad marriages saw this as permission from the church to "buy" (annulments are not cheap!) their way out of a bad marriage and still receive the blessings of the institution they loved and wanted to be a part of.

The Catholic Church is not the only religious institution that buckled under the pressure of the wealthiest of its congregation. But it is a dominant player. Once those who had religious education of any faith began to see the leniency offered by the Catholic Church, they pressured other patriarchal leadership to follow.

Now getting a divorce is not seen as reason for excommunication or the promise of an eternity in hell. Rather it is seen as an escape for a living breathing human being to extract herself from her own brand of living hell. Alcoholism, domestic violence (often hand-in-hand), extramarital affairs, and many other reasons for divorce need not be a death sentence of the spirit. Remember the results of the study that a majority of Boomer women found love within two years after a divorce.

Then there's domestic violence. This private hell was even more insidious when the societal norms were to look the other way. We discovered that physical and emotional violence was a learned behavior passed on from generation to generation. It was a coping mechanism for anger, frustration, and insecurity.

But when the news media became the voice of our social conscience and reported on lives that were taken and children abused, the social conscience began to change. Thanks to the feminist movement of the sixties and seventies, women everywhere said, "Enough."

Women's shelters and social service agencies all across the country began to give voice to those who dared not speak. And so the women's shelters and domestic violence issues made it to the level of state and federal funding agendas. As they educated the public and the law enforcement agencies, the awareness shifted from that of indifference to that of criminal prosecution of the offenders. And it gave those women who had nowhere to go and no one to speak to about it a chance for a new life free of violence and fear of retribution. Now there is no question that divorce is not only an option but a life-saver for those whose lives are affected by domestic violence.

Maybe it's that, as we age, we recognize our own mortality and that the adage "life is too short" has real meaning. Maybe it's the fact that we know ourselves better and know what makes us happy. Maybe it's the awareness that we know the value of slowing down to smell the roses and make our lives simpler. Maybe it's the fact that we are now not willing to tolerate what does not please us since we spent the majority of our lives pleasing others. Whatever the reason, it seems we are being more protective of our right to happiness and less worried about what the world thinks.

If we've managed to keep the love alive with the best husband in the world, we consider ourselves among the precious few. Short of that, marriages that exist because of inertia and fear of change are among the darkest secrets in the world, and without the belief in something better out there, they are destined to just mark time. It's an extraordinary waste of human potential and happiness.

As long as we continue to insist that divorce is a public acknowledgment of failure, with a need to cast blame, and not a private desire for one or two people to find inner peace, the institution of marriage will gradually disappear. Maybe we need something new to replace it.

ACTION STEPS

1. Do the exercise to figure out your current living expenses and see if you are in line with the percentages for the three types of expenses.
2. If you don't already have them, apply for some credit cards (try for one bank credit card) and use them. Please pay off the balance every month.
3. Consider some of your passions that you might turn into income if you need to leave your marital home.

NO FEAR ABOUT GIVING
TO CHARITY

If you could make a difference for two big problems the world faces today, what would they be? For some of you that may be an agonizing decision because you can think of many. For those who can't pick two, think a little harder. War? Cancer? Homelessness? Hunger? Poverty? HIV/AIDS? Domestic violence? Wounded veterans?

In some American families, and now as a requirement of graduation in many high schools, community time is an integral part of life—time to give back to the community that gives you so much.

With a new-found charitable intent in our country, in part because of the many Academy Award–winning movies on such topics, we are making the support of charitable and environmental causes a large part of our culture.

One of the most incredible, but no longer so exceptional, stories I know in the nonprofit world is that of the woman who volunteered on a board of directors knowing that she had the time to help but not the money to contribute. As her tenure on the board increased, and her knowledge of the finances and the annual fund-raising events became legendary, the board convinced her to become the interim executive director of the organization following the sudden death of the current exec.

She fought and fought the board that cajoled her and supported her and finally enrolled her, and she is still the exec director ten years later. She credits her passion for the cause and her willingness to learn what she could while on the board as the reason to stay in the job. She said it gave her the ability to learn some interesting management skills involving negotiating with unions, massaging the egos of the board members, and being held responsible for raising more money each year with the fund-raising initiatives.

The position is something she never aspired to but one that has secured a significant source of income to her family, and not an income she or her husband ever thought would be a part of their lives. There are many women who have turned their passion for a cause into a well-paid position within charities they dearly love. So take a hard look at the next offer you get to volunteer for a board position. You never know where it will lead.

PROMOTING CAUSES BECAUSE

We now know of the need to grow greener in many ways, not just externally, but internally as well. The organic food industry has grown so much that what used to exist on the fringes as a place to go for paranoid food freaks is now a major section of most grocery store chains and is the primary mission of other publicly traded ones such as Whole Foods.

The need to find more sustainable energy sources is now a key component of new building design and residential properties as well. Our need to be less dependent on fossil fuels and gas-guzzling cars has prompted our auto industry to create cars that run on alternative fuels. What had been a "cause" for those who had vision is now becoming mainstream. And that is the intent of most people who have a passion and a burning desire to make change.

There are still causes that linger and those that seemed too remote to care about. So many new ones surface in a world where we are now made aware of them merely because they are thrust in our faces by media coverage. We cannot pretend they don't exist. So although we are making some significant inroads in many issues on our planet, they and many new ones continue to ask for our attention. You will not be without a list to pick from.

If you were raised with no interest in giving back to your community, charitable giving may not be in your blood. But for those who had a different upbringing, the question is not whether to help but where to put your time and resources. By asking yourself the first question in this chapter, you might get a sense of what it is that causes you to "feel" its inequity in your gut.

Without passion for an issue or cause, your desire to help fund an organization's purpose will wane with time. If the issue has affected you or your family directly, then it is usually something you would like to spare others the pain of. Be it cancer, domestic violence, rare diseases, or drug addiction, you know what it costs you and your loved ones beside the dollars and cents. And that may motivate you to want to contribute to a mission so that others can find the resources to avoid the pain you experienced.

Or not.

Perhaps you feel that being involved with these issues just keeps the pain and anguish alive in your life and you would like a break from it. So you find other happier causes to invest your time and money in, such as Big Brothers/Big Sisters where you can one-on-one make a difference in a child's life, and get something back yourself.

Maybe it's the Dress for Success movement that provides clothing and shoes and interviewing skills for women who are in need of these things to get a job and get off the welfare rolls.

Maybe it's the arts, perhaps your local theater or orchestra, that gives you the uplifting and moving feelings of live music or being on stage.

Or the admissions department of your alma mater where you can share your experiences at the college with a young woman who is considering the same school.

If you remember the things you loved to do in your life, see if there is a way for you to participate in that same type of activity with your time and/or your dollars to allow others to find the same joy you did.

GIVING BACK, GETTING BACK

Once you have identified the issues you would like to participate in, the other big question is how to do that. Are there some that you would like to benefit with money or with time or both?

If that issue is national based, such as heart disease or cancer, what is the most effective way to do that? For instance, there are many organizations whose mission it is to eliminate cancer, but should you give to the broader organizations such as the American Cancer Society or to those who support individual types of cancer such as the Susan G. Komen Foundation?

Which organizations are the most efficient at operating costs, leaving more money for the cause, and which are the most effective in generating matching dollars for research to cure the problem? Should you give to a national organization or one in your hometown where you can see the results of the work you do or the money you donate?

Let's find out first how to identify the many organizations around one issue you might be attracted to. For instance, I entered "childhood hunger" in a Google search and found 38 million articles, sites, and organizations related to that cause. If I narrowed the search to organizations in the state where I reside, I would have reduced that considerably. But the point is made that with any cause you can find sites on the Internet that will provide you with information on the causes you hold dear.

Read some of the articles on the subject and find out what organizations' names come up most often. We can take the cynic's stand that their public relations department is really, really good, or we can assume that they are recognized as an institution that has been around for a while and has a fine reputation.

Further research on your computer will allow you to look at the reputation of your favorite charities in your state, under the Department of State. Every nonprofit organization is required to prepare an annual tax return called a Form 990, which tells you everything about the financial health of each charity you might be interested in.

You can find a list of charities in your state committed to the cause you want to support. Don't limit yourself to the state in which you reside. If you are a snowbird and live in a warmer climate for an extended period of time each winter, you might want to check out the same information for the state where you leave the snow and sleet behind.

There are many ways and many avenues to charitable giving. Knowing which is most appropriate for you, your passions, and your financial situation is an important decision you will need to consider before you take some action.

Much research has been done on the idea of charitable giving from the time we developed as a civilization giving scraps of food to the begging poor or the work of the churches to help families without money or shelter. The burgeoning world of institutions both big and small competing for charitable dollars has grown into a mega-industry whose existence before the twentieth century was a blip on the screen compared to what we have today.

The instincts of donors to find a means to make a meaningful contribution has likewise expanded. For those with money and no time, the national organizations offer a simple, clean way to express your interests in their cause with a check or money order. For those with little money and lots of time, the local charities significantly depend on volunteer labor and provide a sorely needed social outlet for many single people. And there is everything in between.

One of the easiest ways to give is to link your purchasing power to a nonprofit organization in your area or a national one. This is so simple even a computer novice can do it. Many sites offer this service, but one I am most familiar with is www.igive.com. This site will allow you to even create a page for your favorite charity if one does not exist on their site. Once you create the page, then you can go to the home page of the site and look for discounts, which will be contributed by the vendor to your charity.

For instance, say you normally do your holiday shopping at online sites such as L.L. Bean, Land's End, or Eddie Bauer. When you go to the igive.com site, you will log in and then go shopping. You can go directly to the website of the retailer, and when you make your purchase, the charity you registered for will automatically receive a check for the discount the retailer offers. These can add up.

If a board of directors, staff, friends, and families were to do this, the amount of the checks to your favorite charity can be substantial. Most retailers give around 3 to 4 percent of your purchase to your charity. Talk about easy! And if you regularly buy online, books, CDs, or other items, the igive site continues to send your rebate directly to your charity. The only thing you must remember to do is sign in to the igive.com website before you shop.

At this time, they have no limit on what amount they will donate. So remember to use this valuable tool.

Some local supermarkets will also donate to your favorite charity based on your total food bill. You must register online with the store, and then if you are a member of their customer discount program, and present your card at checkout, they will automatically send the check to your fave once a month. If the nonprofit makes an attempt to alert all its friends and supporters, this type of automatic giving can really create a significant piece of new revenue for your organization. And it costs them nothing. Even better.

Here are some other ideas:

- If you have managerial experience, your contribution to local causes can include board membership and/or an opportunity to navigate the tricky waters of designing and executing formal fund-raisers.

- You can be a behind-the-scenes worker bee who stuffs envelopes and puts stamps on them to help in an annual campaign.

- You can offer to walk the animals at the local animal shelter and clean their cages.

- You can gather a group of friends for a presentation by the director of development for your favorite cause and have them come with their checkbooks to raise funds.

- If you are a college graduate, you can help them recruit students to your alma mater or help in getting updated contact information from your former classmates.

- You could join some local volunteer organizations if you are still a good driver and deliver meals-on-wheels to shut-ins and have some time to chat with them.

- As a paid caregiver-relief person, you could visit on a regular schedule to homes of those with invalid spouses or parents so that the regular caregiver can get relief or get some time to do personal things.

Volunteering has become a business in and of itself. Many organizations have formal volunteer training programs that you must pass before you can offer your services. But once trained, you are acquiring valuable communication skills, which could turn into a paid position there or somewhere else.

Most every community has a fund established in the memory of a volunteer who gave endless hours to the community. That volunteer learned more on the job than many people do in a paid career. The ability to organize, rally, motivate, delegate, raise funds, mediate personality issues, ask for in-kind contributions from business owners, create work flow schedules, and learn resilience in the face of adversity (such as coping with weather cancellations or negative press) creates a human being with valuable skills.

If you were someone who did this type of nonpaid work and are now looking at where you can use these skills, consider this your invitation to offer your time rather than your money.

To be effective, it does not mean that you need to stay in your community. Doctors without Borders is a national organization that sends physicians as well as other trained medical personnel to under-developed countries to start and train others to staff medical centers for the area's population. This is definitely one-on-one volunteering, but it clearly does not happen in your hometown.

Your hometown has plenty for you to do too. Most towns have an equivalent of a central source for volunteers. They are always looking for people who can offer skills to fit the needs of the community. They serve as a clearinghouse for those social services institutions that need specific types of help and those volunteers who have the experience to fill the need. If your town does not have that type of clearinghouse (or a column in the newspaper), then ask the local religious leaders or your United Way office. They most definitely know where the gaps are.

FOLLOW YOUR PASSION (AND SKILLS)

Charlotte is a retired teacher who has never paid much attention to her finances.

Ever.

She arrived in my office with a box full of statements and envelopes some of which had not been opened. She was talking to a friend the other day and openly admitted her ignorance of her financial affairs and wondered if it really made any difference if she knew what she had or not.

Her teacher's pension and Social Security were more than sufficient to handle her lifestyle needs, including some expensive international travel, so why, she reasoned, should she fix it if it ain't broken? Her friend recommended she have her situation reviewed by a financial professional who could help her and suggested the three of us meet over lunch.

From my perspective it was a delight to have someone in front of me who had more than she needed to support her retirement lifestyle. Yet I knew there was some mischief in not knowing what she had and could even be costing her money by not knowing.

The first thing we did was a review of her experience with money from the time she was a child through her marriages and her divorce. Some interesting patterns came bubbling up: whenever she wanted something she bought it, and the money always seemed to be there to afford it. She treated herself well, did contribute to her retirement plan with some lapses in participation for no reason, and she had no investment strategy other than buying stocks and mutual funds that looked attractive. Not because of their performance, but because she liked the ads.

Then we opened all the envelopes, looked at all the statements, and put them in some logical order. She told us she was sure it didn't amount to much, but she would really like to know what she has and what she should do with it.

That value when we added it up was in excess of $900,000.

When we told her what the number was, she was sure there must be some mistake. We showed her how we came up with the total. She reluctantly agreed with our math.

Now the issue was, how do we reconstruct this portfolio? Surely she did not need any income from it. She always had an excess in her savings account and a guarantee of her pension and her Social Security.

So what is left? I asked her to consider the use of a trust, which would allow the income from the investments to be allocated each year to one or more charities that aligned with her values. She named two that meant something to her.

We set up the trust so that she has control over the assets, but she gets to endow a scholarship for inner city girls every year for a college tuition payment. In addition, she makes a contribution anonymously to the animal shelter in the town she grew up in.

Charlotte is delighted with her new place in the world and loves the idea of being a philanthropist. All because she never opened her envelopes.

If you are more prone to the financial type of charitable giving, then take a look at how your dollars would be most effectively spent. Using the same criteria as discussed earlier, find the community fund that may have been created in honor of its most famous volunteer or, more likely, in the name of its greatest contributor. These foundations exist to fund community works of goodwill but have as many different sets of criteria for funding as there are foundations.

Some will only give to "bricks-and-mortar" projects, meaning they will allow organizations to build buildings, add on extensions, put on a new roof or make some material change. Others will only fund programs that will pay for new staff positions, while others will fund only a new program and specifically deny money for overhead expenses such as rent, utilities, and employee compensation.

Others will provide matching funds for grants from other institutions.

The tax structure of most charitable foundations is that they must disperse at the very least, the income the foundation earns on its investments every year. That may seem like a no-brainer, but they are constantly looking for organizations to provide them with requests to give away the money.

If your chosen organization has a project in need of funding, find the right foundation to submit a proposal to. And where would you go to find out that information? Back to the same sources we all use: Google and Yahoo search engines. Simply type in the name of the "cause" and "Foundations and Grants" and you will be off to the races. There are, of course, organizations that will do the searches for you, prepare the applications and submit them to the appropriate money sources for a fee. How reliable and how effective they are, I can't really say. Just writing the grant applications is a skill in itself that you may find you can do.

Another source of information about the charities you are considering and the resources that exist to get funding for them is the Charity Navigator (www.charitynavigator.org). This website uses a rating table to determine the efficiency of most national and larger state organizations to deliver the services to their constituency.

The ratings table includes four key areas:

1. Program expenses
2. Administrative expenses
3. Fund-raising expenses
4. Fund-raising efficiency

Based on a formula that they explain on their website, they come up with a number of stars to indicate how good the agency is at all of the key areas. Four stars is the best, with one star barely making the grade. The site is a reliable source of information if you are considering donating your money to an organization.

If you have some administrative skills and could volunteer as a working board person, it may show you what organizations could use your help to improve their efficiency. Either way, it's a great source of information.

If you are interested in the same info in your local community, you can volunteer on the allocations panels of your local United Way. These panels review budgets of the organizations the United Way funds with the annual campaign monies they raise. Then they require the community volunteers who serve on these allocation panels to do the same within their smaller segmented groups. Collectively, these panels submit their recommendations for funding to the board of the United Way, and with few exceptions the recommendations of the panels rule the day.

Most organizations that receive funding from their local United Ways are held to task to improve their efficiencies as an organization, and the United Way may withhold funds until these key areas are improved. So if you feel like you have no idea what "cash flow" is, or "return on equity," do not be intimidated. The allocation panels of the United Way offer some basic training in the art of understanding a financial statement.

The more of them you look at (usually four to five agencies in the same area of social services), the more you will become familiar with the statements and the organizations. It is valuable training.

To understand a financial statement is a skill that transcends the mundane and can catapult you to higher and higher levels of board involvement. It is not at the level that you would prepare a financial statement but you begin to understand the relationship between the money the charity spends on overhead (staff, employee benefits, rent, utilities, office supplies) and the money they actually use to fund programs for the population they intend to serve.

The connections you will make in the community are priceless. People from all walks of life volunteer to be on these panels and can become significant resources for you in the future.

HOW CAN YOU HELP?

How do you determine whether you are a worker bee or a board member or anything in between? A well-researched book, *The Seven Faces of Philanthropy,* attempts to help you find yourself in that question. Essentially, the authors, Prince and Maru, have identified seven types of people and recommend the types of organizations and the types of roles you can play in each:

- The Communitarian – doing good makes sense
- The Devout – doing good is God's will
- The Investor – doing good is good business
- The Socialite – doing good is fun
- The Altruist – doing good feels right
- The Repayer – doing good in return
- The Dynast – doing good is a family tradition

Depending on which of these is the most dominant motivation for you to donate either your time or money, the authors outline by chapter the significant characteristics of this type of giver. They then suggest the types of services you would be most suited for along with the types of charities you would be attracted to. I have found the information in this book to be valuable in helping direct clients to places that have the most impact on their charitable intents.

If you find yourself fitting one of these descriptions, then you might have an indication of what type of volunteering you would like to do. If working with causes gets you much more than you give, determine how much time during a week you want to give to these challenges. Many women have complained they got "sucked in" to too many volunteer activities and had no time for the other activities in their busy lives. It is really important that you set some limits on what amount of time and what roles you want to play in your community or national involvement.

If you plan your week around the people and places that are most important in your life, then the time for volunteering may be shorter than you initially think. Even if you let it be known you have some time to work with groups on their many needs, they may become enamored of your work and request more. Women have a hard time saying no. But say it you must.

If you are a working mother, and you determine it is important to spend time with your family, the time you spend on volunteer organizations might be more limited than a woman who is retired and has more free time to devote to the organizations.

If you are retired and decide that working for your favorite organizations is the highlight of your week and gives you a feeling of purpose, then trust that they will find you. Most nonprofit organizations have a greater need for help than there are helpers.

But again, make sure your charities are not your life. A well-balanced life is key to mental and emotional happiness, and too often the charities' needs become so overwhelming that it is hard to deny a request for help. Keep it in perspective.

TAX BENEFITS BACK TO YOU

If you plan on sharing your wealth, how do you determine how much to give? That, of course, is an individual question, but most religious and cultural norms start at 10 percent of your income—a practice known as tithing. This standard has been ideal in helping those who want to give but do not have the faintest idea where to start. For most, during their working lifetimes, this percentage figure works.

Also ready to help is the United Way in most communities. They offer an automatic payroll deduction for those who have a hard time budgeting their desire to give and lack the discipline to do it. You can also set up monthly automatic invoicing to your credit cards so you can split a lump sum into tinier bits (and of course, pay it off at the end of the month!). But keep in mind the overall limit of what you want to contribute and stick to it.

If you have more than enough to make substantial financial contributions, use one of many ways to structure your gifts so that they make sense from both a charitable and financial perspective. Charitable trusts, gifts of appreciated securities (stocks and bonds), gifts of real estate, gifts of life insurance policies, annual gifts, endowment gifts, and many other strategies can make a significant difference in the effect your gift has on your current tax returns as well as its impact to the charity.

Here are a few highlights of these tax-saving strategies. Please know that they are not applicable to everyone and do require a review by your CPA as well as your estate-planning attorney. What may seem like a great idea may not necessarily be advantageous for you from either a tax perspective or from an estate-planning perspective.

Too many times clients may want to benefit a charity that helped play a pivotal role in their own lives to the exclusion of their own financial security and that of a surviving spouse; the emotions are high and the need to guarantee the charity's survival for the future is paramount to them, but the long-term effects of the generous gifts may unintentionally disinherit or impoverish survivors.

So here's how a few people solved both problems:

- Charitable remainder trust. This legal instrument is designed to allow a gift to be made during the lifetime of the donor. The charity then invests the money with the income from the donation given to the donor for as long as he or she lives. It can even be designed so that the income from the trust continues for the spouse or a child for some period of time thereafter. When the donor or the last of its income beneficiaries dies, the original gift plus its interim growth is available to the charity usually for its general use. The donor gets an income tax deduction at the time of the original gift, and the income received by the donor and her beneficiaries is not fully taxable during their lifetimes. Both parties win.

  But the donation must be with funds that the donor does not need for any other basic living expenses or medical conditions because once the gift is made, it cannot be returned to the donor. And it is forever removed from the estate of the donors, meaning the children or other intended heirs will not receive the value of the gift although they can receive the income if the donor intended that when the gift was made.

- Charitable lead trust. This form of trust allows for the reverse of the charitable remainder trust. In this case, the donor allows the charity to use the income generated by the funds immediately and for the life of the donor, with the promise to pay to his or her beneficiaries the remainder in the trust after the donor's death.

  This is a way to help with current income tax problems and to guarantee the asset will return to the family after the death of the donor. The children or other beneficiaries will have to claim it as an inherited asset, but if they are in smaller tax brackets than the parent, the children will supposedly retain more of the asset than the parents would have.

- Grantor retained annuity trust (GRAT). Let's say that you, Mom, are living in a house in your hometown and all your children have moved to other parts of the country or own their own homes in your part of the country. They know that they will not ever want to return to your home to live there for the rest of their lives. In that case, a GRAT would be a perfect gift to a charity because the home could be used to generate some current income to you and a place for your favorite charity to sell sometime in the future. They would get the proceeds of the sale without any income tax, and you would be receiving mostly tax-free income from the charity for the remainder of your life.

  If you died before all the income (annuity) was paid out to you, then your children might be held accountable for the taxes due on the remainder. To really make this work, we assume your children are in lower tax brackets than you are. In all, it is a great way to move real estate out of an otherwise taxable estate and give both the charity and the donor a winning deal. Of course, the charity must be financially capable of paying out the income to you for the rest of your life, so, again, err on the side of caution in asking for the financial stability of the charity before you set up the GRAT.

- Gift of life insurance. Many times we see clients who no longer have a need for a life insurance policy or two. Rather than cash it in and take the money, we have recommended that they donate the insurance policy to their favorite charity (or charities). The charity pays the annual premium to keep the insurance in force, and the donor gets a charitable deduction for the amount of the premiums she paid during her lifetime. The charity receives the insurance money when the donor dies, tax-free, and the donor gets a substantial tax deduction. This tax deduction can be used up in one year or carried over, year to year, until it is depleted to offset current income taxes. The charity gets the use of the cash value of the insurance policy (if the policy was of that type) and can borrow against it for current cash flow needs.

- Gift annuity. If you don't have the kind of wealth that most people associate with major gifts—the type that has your name written all over the doorway or on the building—then perhaps you might want to consider the gift annuity. It is a way to guarantee some retirement income and make a gift to a charity at the same time. This is similar to the charitable remainder trust mentioned earlier but without all the complicated legal paperwork. The gift annuity requires that you give a minimum amount (usually $10,000) to the charity and they in turn promise to pay you a lifetime income based on a fixed rate of return, not unlike a certificate of deposit from a bank. So if the current rates are 3 percent, then you will gift the $10,000 to your favorite charity and they will pay you $300 a year for the rest of your life. Again it presupposes that you will not need the $10,000 CD since you will not be able to get it back, nor will a spouse or children. You do get a tax deduction for the gift but make sure you understand that it is nonreturnable. And the current interest rate the charity commits to is the one you are stuck with for the rest of your life.

The charity is not required to invest the money separately from the rest of its general funds, so if the charity folds, so does your income stream. Some of the larger national charities are not in jeopardy of this happening, but the local ones might be. So again, as suggested earlier in this chapter, do your homework on this one. If it is a local charity that is partially funded by your local United Way, please have a friendly chat with the current executive director and find out how financially stable your favorite charity is before you present them with your funds.

- Gifts of appreciated investments. This is often a very easy
  one for many people. Instead of sending cash or taking
  it out of your paycheck, take a look at your portfolio
  and see if you have some stocks or bonds or other
  assets, such as real estate, you bought many years ago,
  which have significantly increased in value. The money
  you originally paid for the asset and its value now has
  undoubtedly appreciated quite handsomely, despite the
  ups and the downs of the markets. Rather than sell the
  stocks, bonds, or real estate, consider giving the same
  to the charity directly. Because if they are exempt from
  paying income taxes, the charity can take the asset, sell it
  and keep 100 percent of the gains free from taxes.
  If *you* sold the shares of stock or the real estate, you, on
  the other hand, would have to pay taxes on the gains.
  And then, with what was left, you would make the gift.
  Under current law if your gift was an investment asset,
  like a stock, bond, or mutual fund, your donation would
  be valued at the original price you paid for it plus any
  reinvested dividends and capital gains. If it was real estate,
  the value is determined by what you paid for it originally
  plus any improvements you made to it over the years. In
  any event, the deduction is a great one and is usually larger
  than it would be if you sold the asset and then gave the net
  amount to your favorite charity.

- Annual gifts. Most well-managed local charities, as well
  as the larger ones, have an annual fund drive designed
  to raise money from their community for the general
  purposes of paying their overhead expenses. These funds
  are usually a commitment that is presumed to be renewed
  each year by the donor and the charity depends on it for
  their survival.
  The donation usually entails a letter or a phone call thanking
  you for your generous donation last year and telling you
  about all the wonderful things your donation allowed the

charity to do for its clients. The wording of the request usually goes something like this, "So, can we count on your $100 for next year?" And so it goes. This is a general gift and one that you can deduct on your income tax return. Most of us get in the habit of automatically renewing our "pledge" for another year without thinking of the total amount of giving we make. If this was to be repeated with several charities over the course of the year, that total can really add up. Be mindful of this when you say yes.

- Endowments. These are usually gifts made over a period of time, say three to five years. You commit to a total gift amount and make equal periodic payments each year until your commitment is satisfied.

  The endowment is a great way to allow the charity a chance to use your annual payments as matching funds to enable them to leverage your gift to qualify for grants and funds from others. But the downside is that if your commitment was a function of what your investments were doing when you made the pledge and then find that the investments were devalued or you needed the money for other medical or personal emergencies, you are still committed to the charity. There are no formal legal papers saying you are bound by the commitment; it is a matter of personal integrity that calls you to honor the commitment. Sometimes that is not possible, so a call to the director of development or the planned giving department of the charity (maybe to the executive director) to discuss your situation is in order.

  Please do not let a commitment to a charity overrule your need for the assets for personal reasons. An unexpected medical issue or an unemployed spouse, child, or grandchild who is in need of the funds for basic living expenses should trump the commitment to a charity. It happens. Rather than just ignore it and not pay it, a call to the charity would help to reestablish trust between both parties.

This is just a primer of the types of gifts you can make to a charity. Consult with your CPA and/or estate-planning attorney for other combinations of these strategies and some of the more technical types of legal arrangements that are too involved to be discussed here.

Making a gift of your time and money to charities is one of the most rewarding contributions anyone can make to our planet. How you do that is as individual as you are. Consider all the different facets of charitable giving and find some that get your heart racing and those will be the ones that will allow you to make a difference in the world. And Lord knows, we need it.

ACTION STEPS

1. Determine what two causes light you up.
2. See if your money gifts align with those causes and try to make it so.
3. Go online and look up the organizations you give funds to and see how well they rank.

NO FEAR ABOUT INVESTING
IN RETIREMENT PLANS

Marge, who was sixty-two at the time, wanted us to review her investment selections in her company's 401k plan. When we saw what she had invested in, we gasped. Her son told her to put 75 percent of it in an aggressive stock fund and the rest in a money market fund. In essence, he was telling her to be foolishly aggressive.

She had made that selection in the summer of 2007, just a month before the stock market went into a free-fall, and she lost most of what she had saved. The more egregious part of the story is that she expected to retire in three years. We all know of the struggles of the stock market in those subsequent three years. She will probably not be able to live from the money invested in her 401k plan.

Perhaps nothing about employee benefits is more misunderstood and frightening to an employee (or an employer, for that matter) than the selection of investments for their 401k plans. The world of investing that was otherwise left to those who had either the interest in that world or the resources to hire someone who did understand it has now been thrust upon the uninitiated and unsophisticated.

The Feds, in their consummate wisdom, realized the disadvantage it was placing investment knowledge on the uninformed and decided to add a compulsory requirement to the providers of 401k plans: deliver basic investment knowledge to the 401k plan participants so they could make informed decisions as to the most appropriate investment choices offered by the plan. The required education is more often delivered in group settings as a perfunctory, canned presentation facilitated by the organization that "sold" the plan to the employer. Employees who are, by nature, shy and afraid of looking "stupid" usually leave these meetings knowing no more than they did when they came in the door. These meetings should be an earnest attempt to help the participants to find the most suitable investment strategy for their current situation.

To satisfy the federal requirement of educating the participants, the "education" must only be given at the start of the plan; no ongoing education is required. And that is where most people fail at knowing what selection is most appropriate for their current situation, which changes by the year. What is appropriate for a twenty-seven-year-old is not appropriate for a sixty-year-old.

But if the employer (and more often the provider) of the 401k plan does not review the investment selections on at least a bi-annual basis, they are neglecting their duties. And we see clients who are participants in their 401k plan with investment selections that are wholly inappropriate for their risk tolerance or for their age. Too often, it is too late to reverse the effects of their selections since they will not have the time to recover what they lost.

People who do not know what to do with the money they will be contributing to a 401k plan will most likely defer to the recommendations of their assumingly more knowledgeable family members or friends. And we all know the value of "free advice."

If you are feeling like one of these people who knows less after attending a group investment meeting than when you walked in (and you rarely even open the monthly or quarterly statements because you just don't understand what you are looking at), it is your responsibility to contact the plan administrator in your office and request a one-on-one meeting with the plan provider to share your concerns. They are all trained to work with people, either in a group or one-on-one, to discuss your tolerance for risk, your proximity to retirement, and your understanding of the options offered. Ask for this advice.

There is great peril here. And great opportunity at the same time.

START AT THE BEGINNING

So where do you start, and how do you know if you are on the right track? It is like all things new and scary. You have to start at the beginning.

Know a few basic truths about retirement investments:

- Investments in a 401k plan are made with money that is deducted from your paycheck before the income taxes are calculated. That means less of your income is taxed.

- The dividends and interest earned by your investments in the 401k plan are not included in your current tax returns.

- Increases in the value of your investments in a 401k plan are not currently taxed.

- You cannot normally take money from a 401k plan before age fifty-nine and a half.

- If your plan allows it, you can roll over 401k money from a previous employer into your current 401k plan.

- You can take money in the plan as a loan for "hardships," specifically, medical bills, a new home down payment, tuition, or imminent foreclosure on your primary residence. These circumstances, however devastating they may be, will require that your subsequent contributions to your 401k will be used to repay your loan and not to accumulate money for your retirement. And while you are repaying your loan, you are missing out on the matching contributions your employer would have been

making. If your plan allows loans for these purposes, your
request must be approved by a committee or at least the
administrator. The interest you will pay is usually pegged
to the current prime lending rate (a rate reserved for
those with the best credit scores). Borrowing from your
401k should be considered the last place you will go to
find money: you are forfeiting the years of accumulation
in your 401k that will have a huge impact on how much
money you will have at retirement.

• When you retire, you have three choices of how to take
the money in your 401k nest egg: (1) an annuity (a
promise to pay you and/or your spouse an income for
your lives based on your normal life expectancy); (2) a
lump sum payout, which will require that the income
taxes be withdrawn before the check is paid to you; or (3)
a rollover to a special IRA that will allow you to determine
how much and when you want to take the income or
invade the principal once you retire. In the latter, the
IRS says that you must pay the income tax on whatever
amount you withdraw, but the remainder in the rollover
IRA stays untaxed until you withdraw it.

• You *must* begin taking money from your IRAs (rollover
or any other type) when you reach age seventy and a half
and every year thereafter. The annual amount you must
take is based on an IRS formula.

Okay, so now let's get to the meat of it.

For the number of years you will be contributing to your
retirement plan, the investment selection will be the most critical
of all the decisions you make as a participant. Whether you invest
the maximum amount you are allowed by law, or some lesser
percentage, the investments and their performance are key.

For example, the investment most people use in their 401k
plans is the stable value fund. It may be called by different
names, like the guaranteed fund or the fixed income fund,
but in essence, they all carry the same type of investments:

certificates of deposit (CDs), money market funds (MMFs), or U.S. Treasury securities, such as treasury notes or treasury bonds or bonds of government agencies, such as the Federal Home Loan Board, GNMA, or FNMA. Occasionally, there may be some mortgages thrown in, especially if the custodian of the plan is an insurance company. Expect no growth here, just income. And if this fund needs to keep the money in investments such as these, then expect little to no earnings in today's environment.

But, people will argue, they are safe.

Until they're not. Remember the recent near collapse of GNMA (Ginnie Mae mortgages) or FNMA (Fannie Mae mortgages)? The current government securities, treasury notes and bonds, are paying virtually nothing in interest income.

So how will your money grow to help you maintain financial security for the rest of your life?

The most heinous of all situations is to find yourself outliving your money. I have seen that happen to well-meaning people. They want to be invested in what they think is safe, when in fact their investments are risky. Keeping all your money in the type of stable investment just mentioned is a blueprint for disaster.

So how do you sleep at night and still invest for your retirement? You stir up the pot. You put some money in the stable value fund and the rest of it in a carefully sculpted mix of different asset classes.

It's time again for a primer. Call it Investment 101.

Many years ago, a sage man named Dr. Harry Markowitz proved that the majority of excellent investment results were not a matter of picking the right stock at the right time, but of having your investments well diversified.

This degree of diversification would allow the investment portfolio to ride through the ups and the downs of the investment cycle expecting to minimize the downturns and maximize the upturns without experiencing the extremes. His theory did not intend to make people believe they would never see the value of their investments go down, nor that they would always go up, but that, in investing *with* his theory, the downs would be less severe and the ups would not hit the stratosphere. And his theory has maintained its efficacy for over fifty years. We have all tweaked it by adding some new asset classes that did not exist when Dr. Markowitz created the model, but in essence, the logic still survives.

What asset classes should be represented in a well-constructed portfolio? There are primarily three: cash, fixed income, and equities. All others are subcategories of these three. For the most part, there is no value in keeping *cash* in a 401k since it will never be needed for an emergency. The exception to that rule is if the stock and bond markets are so bad, a money manager may consider selling same and putting the money in cash until things improve. That did happen in the last two years.

Let's take a time out for another lesson, Investment 102. Definitions would help.

A bond is a loan made between you, as the lender, and some entity or institution, as the borrower. It carries with it a promise to return your money at some point in time in the future. And for that loan, they will pay you a stated annual amount of interest, usually divided by two and paid out semi-annually. Once the term of the loan is over, you get your money back. No more, no less. But the income from the bond is taxable as interest income. If the "borrower" (also known as the "issuing entity" or simply the "issuer") is a municipality or a municipal authority, like a sewer authority, a hospital, or a school district, the interest on the bond may be tax-free. At times, the issuer of the bond is allowed to pay it all back earlier than the stated time if they feel they can find others to buy the bonds with a lower interest rate. In that case, you may find you have the loan repaid to you before you expected it. That would force you to then go back to the bond market and find another bond with hopefully a better interest rate than the one you had. It can be tricky, which is why most people prefer to use money managers to buy and sell those bonds.

A *stock*, on the other hand, is a piece of ownership in a company that issues the stock. You can own a piece of McDonald's, Lowe's, Bank of America, or other public company. As the company's fortunes ebb and flow, so does the value of your stock. But there are so many companies to invest in, it is virtually impossible to pick the right one at the right time, every time.

For most people, and especially those who invest in a 401k plan, the method of choice to access this wonderful world of stock investing is to buy shares of a *mutual fund*. A mutual fund is a collective of investors all of whom can purchase different amounts of the fund, in the form of "shares" of the fund. The fund manager is given a specific directive by the trustees of the fund to invest in certain types of assets, and no others.

Mutual funds can hold both stocks and bonds in one fund or be as narrowly defined as, for example, owning only stocks of Japan. Again, knowing how much to put into what types of funds is key to the performance of your 401k.

So let's start with *fixed income investments*. This category has many types of assets that can be very solid investments and, at the same time, also very risky. Most people associate fixed income with bonds, and the two terms are used interchangeably. But bonds can be on a spectrum from the most secure, such as U.S. Treasury assets, to junk bonds, which carry the possibility of default (the loss of all the money invested). As you move up the spectrum, the risk increases and so does the interest income generated by the bond. It is notably justified that the higher the risk you take, the more you should be compensated. So a U.S. Treasury might pay 3 percent interest, while a junk bond could pay 10 percent. And everything in between.

In addition to the bonds in the fixed income category, there are mortgage backed bond funds, junk bond funds, international bond funds, global bond funds and emerging market bond funds. All of these have a place in the category called "fixed income" or just "bonds." If you have these choices in your 401k, then a quick look at what percentage you allocate to each type is appropriate. That depends on your age and proximity to retirement.

GOLDEN RULES FOR GOLDEN YEARS

One golden rule is have more than 50 percent of your assets in "bonds" by the time you reach retirement so as to stabilize the income stream for your living expenses in your golden years, but again, that depends. It depends on your earning capacity after you retire, the timing of your Social Security retirement benefits, your pension payments, and more. So don't take to heart the golden rule unless you have discussed this with a professional.

In the equity category, the sky is the limit. And sometimes the floor falls out beneath you. The range of possibilities is endless in this category, but equities should be a significant part of every retirement investment plan. The reason for this is simple: the income stream from fixed income/bonds is just that, fixed. If your lifestyle needs increase due to inflation or other medical or lifestyle changes, you cannot invade the principal of your fixed income investments to provide that additional money. If you take a lump sum from the fixed income portfolio, you are lessening the ability of the portfolio to produce the income you are used to living on. The bond portfolio is designed to generate income, not to grow.

So the growth must come from the equity side of the portfolio. That is usually associated with stocks. But just as bonds come in many different shapes and sizes, so, too, do equities. Equities include stocks, but can include natural resources (stocks of companies that mine or drill oil, gas, gold, silver, for example) and real estate (stocks of national builders, commercial property owners such as malls, office buildings, parking garages).

In a 401k plan, these privately owned assets (real estate, gold, oil) are not permitted. They will not be seen in the list of available investment choices, unless they are all held in a mutual fund that invests in these types of investments. Furthermore, most 401k plans do not get that prolific in their investment choices. Knowing what percentage to invest in the larger, broader categories will probably suffice.

So how can you determine what that percentage is? Try this: subtract from 100 your age and use that as a rule to determine how much should be in bonds. If you are fifty-five years old, then you should have 55 percent in bonds and 45 percent in stocks. It doesn't always work, but this formula is a starting point. As you age, using this formula, you should be changing your allocation each year until you retire. If this is the only investment you have for retirement, then the rule is not a bad place to start.

If, however, you have outside investments, especially in real estate or other non-liquid investments, like a closely held business, then you must consider all of this in your allocation of 401k funds.

To further complicate the issue, know you are limited by your employer's investment choices as to which mutual funds you can invest in. It would be nice to want to create a well-diversified portfolio, but if you have only three choices, our theories of asset allocation will live as just a good idea.

If you do have a considerable number of 401k investment choices, if you are age fifty-five, have no other investment portfolios to consider, then a well-diversified 401k plan might look like this:

Cash

			0%
Fixed Income			
	U.S. Government Bond Fund	30%	
	U.S. Corporate Bond Fund	20%	
	International Bond Fund	3%	
	Emerging Markets Bond Fund	2%	
	TOTAL		55%
Equities			
	U.S. Large Cap Stock Fund	25%	
	U.S. Small Cap Stock Fund	15%	
	International Stock Fund	3%	
	Emerging Markets Stock Fund	2%	
	TOTAL		45%
TOTAL ALLOCATION			100%

Please note that this example is not cast in concrete and is not intended to be providing investment advice. It is simply a rough draft of what a well-diversified 401k plan would look like if your employer had funds like this available for you.

Two caveats: rather than rebalance this portfolio every year to the formula (100 minus your current age in bonds, the rest in equities), consider rebalancing every three to five years. If you did so every year, you would not be allowing your investments to recover in down markets.

Second, if your employer does not allow for all these funds, round up to the next highest percentage category. For instance, if you do not have international stock funds to pick from, put that same allocation proportionately to the U.S. Small Cap Fund and the U.S. Large Cap Fund. Please know: the fund names may not be a match to those I have included here, but if you look at the information about the funds before you select them, you will see those terms used in the description of the fund. Stay with that. *Or better yet, contact your 401k provider and ask for assistance.*

Another easy way to select your 401k investments is to buy into the lifestyle funds. These funds can be called by many different names, but essentially they leave the driving to the mutual fund managers. They will carry a date in the name of the fund, like Lifestyle Fund 2015, 2020, 2025, and so on. In these funds, the money managers move the allocation to the bond side as you age and do so every five years. That way, you need not be concerned about the decision as to when and where to place the money. Or maybe you should be more involved?

We have seen the money managers of these funds stray somewhat from the allocations necessary for stability in favor of getting a better-than-average performance. And what's wrong with that, you ask? You are taking on too much risk at a time when economic conditions may suggest less of it. If the money managers think there may be a "bond bubble," like the "housing bubble" we all experienced, they may decide to move you out of bonds all together and go to cash.

If the "bond bubble" never materializes, then you will have to accept the lower bond interest rates when the managers decide to take the cash and buy whatever bonds are now for sale. These lifestyle funds have performed okay, but that is the risk you assume when you allow others you don't know to make those investment decisions for you. Still, it is better than having all your money in the stable value fund—a misnomer if ever there was one!

An important disclaimer: You have to align your investment portfolio to your level of risk. If you are someone who cannot stand to see even a temporary decline in your 401k values, then you should raise the level of the bond allocation. But if you do that, you also raise the risk that you might outlive your money. You must trade off your temporary fears for the longer-term stability of having enough income to live the life you want.

On the other hand, if you are someone who believes the only way to live the life you want is to invest 100 percent of your money in stocks, you need a reality check too. When you make a decision to allocate your money, be it the same as the sample, or a different one, know what your true risks are. There is a huge difference between safety and stability. And most people confuse the two.

THE JOY OF STABILITY

Let's explain the difference: *Stability* is the ability to pay your living expenses in any economic environment. Safety is the ability to depend on a guaranteed amount of income at any time. On the face of it, it would appear that safety is the way to go. Although it is tempting, it is an illusion.

The safety of your investments gives you a false sense of security that you will be able to generate enough income to equal your expenses. That's a great feeling! Until inflation starts to rear its ugly head and forces you to tap into that same bucket of money to pay for higher electric prices, higher food prices, higher gasoline prices, and higher real estate taxes.

Once you take money from your portfolio of CDs, bonds, stable value funds, and other safe investments, you now reduce the amount of principal to be invested. The less available to be invested, the less income it can generate. Two options remain: (1) take the lower amount of principal and invest it in higher interest bonds, which carry a higher potential for default (inability to pay you the income or to return your money when the bond matures); or (2) live with a lower amount of income for the foreseeable future.

At some point, the expenses become fixed and you cannot reduce your spending any more. So you sell your home, move in with your children or into an apartment, and now use the proceeds of your home sale to generate income. Until the landlord raises the rent, the car needs to be replaced, the medical costs go above and beyond the Medicare increase. Then you are forced to once again dip into the principal of your portfolio to pay the extra costs. Or you buy riskier bonds to get the higher interest rates, or you buy CDs that are due to mature in more than five years so you can get the higher interest rates. And the drama starts all over again.

I would prefer stability to safety. And I am sure most of you would as well. But until someone explains it to you, you take the road of least volatility and opt for the fixed income route. Most people associate fixed income assets with stability. The truth is, they are the opposite.

To determine how much stability and how much safety you need, most investment professionals will ask you to complete a risk profile. These are a series of questions designed to determine how you would react to a decrease in the value of your investments over the short term (six months or less) and over the long term (one year or more). The questions are also looking for your reaction to how oriented you are to short-term fluctuations versus the possibility of long-term gains. And how soon you would need the money to generate income versus how many years you have until you expect to retire. And many variations on this theme.

If done correctly, the end result is a numeric profile, which will help you determine how much, within a range, should be in stocks and how much should be in bonds. Then the professional from the 401k plan should help you determine how much in each subcategory should be allocated to each, like the model shown earlier in this chapter.

This exercise must be repeated at least every five years. Your investment model, if you chose other than the "lifestyle funds," must be adapted to the changes of your answers to the risk profile. Obviously, you are now closer to retirement than you were five years ago, and your tolerance for investing in bonds or stocks may have changed, and you will have a larger pot of money to work with since you have been making contributions for the last five years and, hopefully, your employer has been making matching contributions.

FREE MONEY

Did you know that your employer may be committed to making a matching contribution to your account at least once a year? Depending on which format the company used, you could have a match more often than that and in many different percentages. If they opt for the easiest, that could be a match of 3 percent of your salary once a year. The 3 percent assumes you will contribute the maximum of 6 percent of your salary and they will match 50 percent (or 3%).

Unfortunately, too many people fail to make the full contribution and so in essence they miss the free money (employer match) given to the participants who do contribute the full 6 percent. In some plans, the employer will match any percentage up to 6 percent. Please check this out with your plan administrator.

There are always reasons not to contribute the full 6 percent, but I have yet to hear a really good one.

Sure I understand there are demands on your salary: medical premiums (if you share that cost with your employer), taxes, charitable contributions, your family's activities, needs, medicines, co-pays on your health insurance, and any number of other expenses.

Those pale in comparison to the lack of funds when you retire. You can buy used equipment for the kids and grandkids, lease or finance a car, refinance a mortgage, but you can't finance retirement. Buy generic, eat out less often, do without the finest vacations, find ways to compromise, but please do not pass up this chance to have half of your contributions matched. That is a 50 percent return on your investment before it even gets invested!

The full 6 percent contribution may or may not be available to you. If you are in a class of "highly compensated employees" (business owners, senior-level executives), you may not be allowed to contribute the maximum percentage if doing so would make the 401k plan "top-heavy." *Top-heavy* is a term the Feds use to describe a plan that has less than 75 percent of the eligible employees contributing.

You, as a highly compensated employee, would be penalized by being allowed to contribute only the amount that the formula allows, something less than 6 percent. This is why you want your fellow employees to participate to the max, if possible.

The government, realizing what slackers we are, also gave us a chance to increase that percentage contribution (regardless of the top-heavy restrictions) with a flat amount of $5,500 if we are over the age of fifty. So you can add more to that retirement fund to "catch-up" every year until you cease employment. In some cases, employers will match that amount too. I hope you have asked your employer about that by now.

There really are no steadfast rules for how much you should put into your retirement plans. At least start out with 2 to 3 percent. Some plans now make it mandatory that the percentage of your contribution will automatically increase by a full percent every year. And if you do not make a decision as to which investment choice(s) you will make, they have a default one for you.

We may resist this type of forced participation, but in the end, it will serve us all well. If you were counting on the federal government to supply you with Social Security payments for the rest of your life, think again. This system is not one that gives you credit for what you contributed over your lifetime; it actually counts on your working to fund the current benefits for those who are now receiving benefits. As that working population declines relative to the number of retirees, the contributions going in to fund those expecting the benefits is declining as well. So please see the urgency of funding your own retirement by generously contributing to your 401k plan.

Don't forget the stragglers! The 401k plans you may have started and contributed to for a few months or years earlier in your career. Your current employer may allow you to roll them over into your existing plan. Check with your administrator.

Or if you don't like the investment choices in your current plan, roll those stragglers into an IRA Rollover Account. Nothing says you have to put it in your current plan. At least get it somewhere where you can get your hands on it and consider it part of your retirement planning.

Regina and her husband were considering retirement in a few years and both had enjoyed substantial accumulations of company stock and mutual funds in their 401k plans. Before Regina started working with her current employer, she had a five-year stint at a law firm and was a participant in her former employer's 401k plan. She knew she used to get an annual statement from them but since she moved out of state, she realized she forgot to send them a change of address. She contacted the old law firm and found that firm was merged with another regional firm. So she contacted the new firm, and with some serious sleuthing, she was able to find her 401k account.

It had doubled in size since she left it there. She then filed the paperwork with the new administrator of the plan to move it to a rollover IRA. She thanked me profusely for reminding her of this, since this money would allow the world cruise to happen. They were both excited about this good news.

I WANT MY MONEY NOW

Now that you have contributed and are reaching retirement age, how do you get at this money? Several ways:

- Pay all the income taxes you would owe and take the remainder in a check. Not a bad idea if you have less than $5,000 in your plan. This amount should not force you into a higher tax bracket so it might make sense. On the other hand, if your 401k is approaching several hundred thousand dollars or more, by cashing it in, you are forcing yourself into a higher tax bracket that could cost you plenty to pay to Uncle Sam before you get yours. In general, this is the worst of the three options.

- Sell all your investments in the plan and roll it over into an IRA. The current custodian of the 401k plan sends a check to your new custodian of the IRA and it is a seamless transaction. Once the money hits the new IRA, you and your advisor decide what investments are best for you at this point. You now become the money manager of your retirement account. This allows you and your advisor to purposely allocate the money to different pools of money for your retirement trips, buying a second home, and other choices. It becomes part of the mix of all your investment funds so you can take advantage of the tax benefits of IRAs and noninvestment accounts in a strategic plan. This is the most desirable of all the options.

- Use the funds to purchase an annuity for you (and your spouse). Although this is not advisable, many retirees have succumbed to the sales presentations of those selling these annuities. And they then regret it. The annuities are loaded with fees from the insurance companies who sell them and many of them are heavily ingrained with fees you will never see. If you want to get out of an annuity, be forewarned. The price is very steep. PLEASE READ ALL THE FINE PRINT BEFORE YOU BUY ONE.

I was very sad to have to tell two hard-working folks who came to see me a few months ago that I could not help them with the annuities they bought two years ago. The annuities were still in the period where back-end charges would apply if they tried to cancel them. The charges were 8 percent on each of the three annuities they bought. They also would have to repay a percentage of the first year's 7 percent interest rate they enjoyed. Because they did not hold the annuities for at least six years, this partial surrender charge applied. In all it would have cost them at least $75,000 in back-end charges to get out. And of course, they had no recollection of the agent telling them that. That is not to say he did not, but they did not remember any conversation on that subject.

401ks are a real gift to the American public. The only disadvantage is not enough people use them. As is human nature, we start thinking about retirement somewhere in our fifties, if then. And it is too late then to amass what we will need to sustain our current lifestyles into retirement.

If you have not participated in a 401k, please do so. If you are participating, up the percentage to the highest your plan will allow, including the "catch-up" provision.

ACTION STEPS

1. Review your 401k plan selections in light of the formula discussed in this chapter (100 minus your age). See if it is appropriate for you given your other investments and risk tolerance.
2. Consider all your previous employers and see if you can discover any 401k plans you left behind. If so, contact the plan administrator and get them rolled over into an IRA Rollover Account for yourself.
3. Consider the concept of safety versus security. Decide which is more important to you.

YOUR FEARLESS ACTION PLAN

In all, if we spent as much time shopping for a trusted financial guide as we did for our holiday gifts, we would all be in greater control of our finances.

Women would not fear being alone whether through divorce or death of a spouse or more easily make the choice not to marry in the first place. We would not place an unequal burden on the men in our lives to handle the financial issues and then complain when it doesn't go the way we wanted. We could teach our daughters to depend on themselves first, and then invite a man or woman to join them in a long-term relationship.

We could take our place on boards of directors of *Fortune 500* companies and know the intricacies of a financial statement. Why we could even run for President of the United States and be assured we could read and understand the national budget! We could invest large sums of money in growing businesses and negotiate loan terms with banks and other private venture capital groups.

We could do a lot and not give up our roles as mothers, wives, daughters, aunts, sisters, sisters-in-law, granddaughters, nieces, and significant others. We can still be caretakers and learn to hire those whose businesses offer such services to make our lives easier without the guilt. We can allow ourselves to live our happiest lives without the fear of having no roof over our heads if we choose to divorce or never marry. We could survive job loss and retirement. We can go about our business, literally, with the desire to make it more successful than just something to pay the bills and keep our heads above water.

In short, we can aspire to greatness in every part of our lives simply by understanding, and using, money to pave the path. It does not need to be our own money. Once we understand how to use other people's money in a disciplined way and go back for more to finance our expansion, we can join the ranks of those whose fortunes were made by overcoming the lack of funds.

Our happiness quotient will increase dramatically too. Knowing we have the resources to live a comfortable, fulfilling life will give us peace of mind—a state few people ignorant of money will ever achieve.

We know that we can make a difference in the world if we have the skills and knowledge of money. The web is replete with sites that ask for contributions for good; women are attracted to them. We know we want to support the kinds of nurturing, good-for-the-next-generation, novice women businesses around the world, but we rarely have the opportunity to see those businesses. The web brings them to us. We are now savvy enough to look at the opportunities, evaluate them and contribute whether it be with time or money, or both.

So now that you have all this knowledge, where do you start on your path to financial peace of mind?

Exactly where you are.

Start by checking out the chapter on how to find a financial advisor. And begin a relationship with a trusted advisor. I hope she will be the best investment you've ever made.

Remind yourself of the action steps after each chapter and use them as a checklist to get yourself prepared for a good conversation with an advisor.

And if you are so inclined, consider starting a Money Circle with some friends who might be interested in talking about money but were too afraid to admit their own ignorance. You can be the facilitator and bring along this book.

Better yet, make them all buy this book and get involved in the process themselves before they attend a Money Circle. Remember the story of the millionth circle. We need to have all women get some basic knowledge of finances so we can declare the millionth circle has begun.

Sara is a physician who has been a subspecialist for many years. She practiced in our area and near a large metropolitan area to supplement her income. She was passionate about women understanding their bodies and how our eating, exercising, and drug use affected our mental and physical health. She was considered by her peers to be somewhat of an oddity, preferring to go it alone so often because she mistrusted the traditional dispensing of drugs to cure all the ills of womankind.

She came to see me because she said she had no time to manage all this and she trusted another woman to help her. As she left the office, she said, "Where were you ten years ago when I could have used your help in doing this right from the start?"

Don't waste another ten years in your life. Start today to understand how money works, and if you are not comfortable with the person you are working with, look for another. We all have personalities, we all have lives outside the office, and we may or may not make you feel as if there is a fit. Keep trying until you find a trusted advisor.

Remember, there is another generation or two behind you. Do not allow them to repeat the same mistakes we Baby Boomer women made. Even if your daughters, granddaughters, nieces, or daughters-in-law can't seem to muster the interest, find ways to make it fun. Their financial future is on the line. Don't fail them.

ACTION STEPS

1. Complete the action steps from all the previous chapters.
2. Make an appointment with a few financial planners in your area and take the checklist with you for the interview. (If you haven't done so already!)
3. Begin to speak to other women you know about getting together in a Money Circle. You'll all be happy you did.

ACKNOWLEDGMENTS

First, I thank my clients, who have honored me with their trust and confidence, especially during the difficult times. And to Aldonna Ambler who first suggested I consider writing this book, interviewed my clients to give me some words and context to describe their relationship with me, and, as an author herself, gave me the encouragement to keep going after some lapses from grace.

Let me acknowledge the many professionals in various fields, not just financial, who have confidentially shared their clients' stories with me, which makes this book all the more real.

Sincere thanks to my friends who have always seen this book as a done deal. To my mom and dad who gave me the life experiences that stayed with me in order to write this book, and to my sister and brother, my cousins and all my family who believe I am more than I think I am.

Special thanks to Eleanor Blayney, Peg Downey, and Elizabeth Jetton from *Directions for Women* who inspired me to take this on and take a stand for women being financially literate.

And special thanks to my husband, Patrick A. di Napoli, whose love and encouragement gave me the impetus to keep writing when I thought I had used up all the Muse had given me.

ABOUT THE AUTHOR

Lynn S. Evans is a Certified Financial Planner®. She specializes in providing personal financial advice for women who are experiencing transitions in their lives: divorce, retirement, widowhood, or career change.

For more than thirty years, as President and CEO of Northeastern Financial Consultants, Inc., a Fee-Only® financial planning firm in Clarks Summit, Pennsylvania, Lynn has used her expertise to help clients know their worth, own their wealth, and enjoy their lives.

Her passion for making a difference in the lives of the women she serves motivated her to develop Money Circles, a series of structured, conversational meetings for women to bridge the gap between having no knowledge of personal finance, to gaining the confidence to successfully work with a financial advisor. She encourages women to have a happy, healthy relationship with money.

Lynn is active in her community. She co-hosts the popular WILK radio series, The Laurie and Lynn Show (a Podcast series), and serves on many community and civic boards. The recipient of the Governor's Top 50 Women in Business in Pennsylvania, she serves as a charter member and current officer of the local chapter of the National Association of Women Business Owners.

She and her husband, Patrick A. di Napoli, enjoy boating, swimming, and playing tennis at their home in the Pocono Mountains of Pennsylvania.

Contact the author: Lynn publishes a popular electronic newsletter and financial advice blog. Readers are invited to subscribe at www.LynnSEvans.com. She is available to speak on the power of the purse to women's and other civic and church groups. Email her at lynn@LynnSEvans.com.

64149356R00130

Made in the USA
Lexington, KY
30 May 2017